VENTRESS MEMORIAL LIBRARY (MARSHFIELD)

P9-CEH-672

DISCARDED

Biog.
WALKER
Gentry

11 X 02

VENTRESS MEMORIAL LIBRARY
LIBRARY PLAZA
MARSHFIELD, MA 02050

DISCARDED

ALICE
WALKER

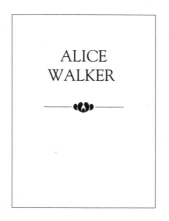

ALICE WALKER

❦

Tony Gentry

Senior Consulting Editor
Nathan Irvin Huggins
Director
W.E.B. Du Bois Institute for Afro-American Research
Harvard University

CHELSEA HOUSE PUBLISHERS
New York   Philadelphia

JUN 0 3 1999

"The Kiss" and "South: The Name of Home" from *Once*, copyright ©1968 by Alice Walker, reprinted by permission of Harcourt Brace Jovanovich, Inc.

"My Daughter Is Coming" from *Horses Make a Landscape Look More Beautiful*, copyright ©1979 by Alice Walker, reprinted by permission of Harcourt Brace Jovanovich, Inc.

"He Said" from *Good Night Willie Lee, I'll See You in the Morning* by Alice Walker. Copyright ©1979 by Alice Walker. Used by permission of Doubleday, a division of Bantam Doubleday Dell Publishing Group, Inc.

"Once, Again" from *Her Blue Body Everything We Know*, copyright ©1991 by Alice Walker, reprinted by permission of Harcourt Brace Jovanovich, Inc.

Chelsea House Publishers
Editor-in-Chief Richard S. Papale
Managing Editor Karyn Gullen Browne
Copy Chief Philip Koslow
Picture Editor Adrian G. Allen
Art Director Maria Epes
Assistant Art Director Howard Brotman
Manufacturing Director Gerald Levine
Systems Manager Lindsey Ottman
Production Coordinator Marie Claire Cebrián-Ume

Black Americans of Achievement
Senior Editor Richard Rennert

Staff for ALICE WALKER
Copy Editor David Carter
Editorial Assistant Nicole Greenblatt
Designer Diana Blume
Picture Researcher Diana Gongora
Cover Illustration Patti Oleon

Copyright © 1993 by Chelsea House Publishers, a division of Main Line Book Co. All rights reserved. Printed and bound in the United States of America.

First Printing

1 3 5 7 9 8 6 4 2

Library of Congress Cataloging-in-Publication Data
Gentry, Tony.
    Alice Walker, author/by Tony Gentry
        p. cm.—(Black Americans of achievement)
    Includes bibliographical references and index.
    Summary: Examines the life and work of the author of "The Color Purple" and other works which focus on the lives of black women.
    ISBN   0-7910-1884-9
            0-7910-1913-6 (pbk.)
    1. Walker, Alice, 1944– —Biography—Juvenile literature. 2. Afro-American authors—20th century—Biography—Juvenile literature. [1. Walker, Alice, 1944– . 2. Authors, American. 3. Afro-Americans—Biography.] I. Title. II. Series.
PS3573.A425Z65 1993   92-5302
813'.54—dc20   CIP
[B]   AC

Frontispiece: Alice Walker in front of Reynolds Cottage on the grounds of Spelman College in 1990.

CONTENTS

BLACK AMERICANS OF ACHIEVEMENT

HENRY AARON
baseball great

KAREEM ABDUL-JABBAR
basketball great

RALPH ABERNATHY
civil rights leader

ALVIN AILEY
choreographer

MUHAMMAD ALI
heavyweight champion

RICHARD ALLEN
*religious leader and
social activist*

MAYA ANGELOU
author

LOUIS ARMSTRONG
musician

ARTHUR ASHE
tennis great

JOSEPHINE BAKER
entertainer

JAMES BALDWIN
author

BENJAMIN BANNEKER
scientist and mathematician

AMIRI BARAKA
poet and playwright

COUNT BASIE
bandleader and composer

ROMARE BEARDEN
artist

JAMES BECKWOURTH
frontiersman

MARY MCLEOD BETHUNE
educator

JULIAN BOND
civil rights leader and politician

GWENDOLYN BROOKS
poet

JIM BROWN
football great

BLANCHE BRUCE
politician

RALPH BUNCHE
diplomat

STOKELY CARMICHAEL
civil rights leader

GEORGE WASHINGTON
CARVER
botanist

RAY CHARLES
musician

CHARLES CHESNUTT
author

JOHN COLTRANE
musician

BILL COSBY
entertainer

PAUL CUFFE
merchant and abolitionist

COUNTEE CULLEN
poet

ANGELA DAVIS
civil rights leader

BENJAMIN DAVIS, SR., AND
BENJAMIN DAVIS, JR.
military leaders

SAMMY DAVIS, JR.
entertainer

FATHER DIVINE
religious leader

FREDERICK DOUGLASS
abolitionist editor

CHARLES DREW
physician

W. E. B. DU BOIS
scholar and activist

PAUL LAURENCE DUNBAR
poet

KATHERINE DUNHAM
dancer and choreographer

DUKE ELLINGTON
bandleader and composer

RALPH ELLISON
author

JULIUS ERVING
basketball great

JAMES FARMER
civil rights leader

ELLA FITZGERALD
singer

MARCUS GARVEY
black nationalist leader

JOSH GIBSON
baseball great

DIZZY GILLESPIE
musician

PRINCE HALL
social reformer

W. C. HANDY
father of the blues

WILLIAM HASTIE
educator and politician

MATTHEW HENSON
explorer

CHESTER HIMES
author

BILLIE HOLIDAY
singer

JOHN HOPE
educator

LENA HORNE
entertainer

LANGSTON HUGHES
poet

ZORA NEALE HURSTON
author

JESSE JACKSON
civil rights leader and politician

MICHAEL JACKSON
entertainer

JACK JOHNSON
heavyweight champion

JAMES WELDON JOHNSON
author

SCOTT JOPLIN
composer

BARBARA JORDAN
politician

CORETTA SCOTT KING
civil rights leader

MARTIN LUTHER KING, JR.
civil rights leader

SPIKE LEE
filmmaker

REGINALD LEWIS
entrepreneur

ALAIN LOCKE
scholar and educator

JOE LOUIS
heavyweight champion

RONALD MCNAIR
astronaut

MALCOLM X
militant black leader

THURGOOD MARSHALL
Supreme Court justice

TONI MORRISON
author

CONSTANCE BAKER
MOTLEY
*civil rights leader
and judge*

ELIJAH MUHAMMAD
religious leader

EDDIE MURPHY
entertainer

JESSE OWENS
champion athlete

SATCHEL PAIGE
baseball great

CHARLIE PARKER
musician

GORDON PARKS
photographer

ROSA PARKS
civil rights leader

SIDNEY POITIER
actor

ADAM CLAYTON
POWELL, JR.
political leader

COLIN POWELL
military leader

LEONTYNE PRICE
opera singer

A. PHILIP RANDOLPH
labor leader

PAUL ROBESON
singer and actor

JACKIE ROBINSON
baseball great

DIANA ROSS
entertainer

BILL RUSSELL
basketball great

JOHN RUSSWURM
publisher

SOJOURNER TRUTH
antislavery activist

HARRIET TUBMAN
antislavery activist

NAT TURNER
slave revolt leader

DENMARK VESEY
slave revolt leader

ALICE WALKER
author

MADAM C. J. WALKER
entrepreneur

BOOKER T. WASHINGTON
educator and racial spokesman

IDA WELLS-BARNETT
civil rights leader

WALTER WHITE
civil rights leader

OPRAH WINFREY
entertainer

STEVIE WONDER
musician

RICHARD WRIGHT
author

ON
ACHIEVEMENT

Coretta Scott King

BEFORE YOU BEGIN this book, I hope you will ask yourself what the word *excellence* means to you. I think that it's a question we should all ask, and keep asking as we grow older and change. Because the truest answer to it should never change. When you think of excellence, perhaps you think of success at work; or of becoming wealthy; or meeting the right person, getting married, and having a good family life.

Those important goals are worth striving for, but there is a better way to look at excellence. As Martin Luther King, Jr., said in one of his last sermons, "I want you to be first in love. I want you to be first in moral excellence. I want you to be first in generosity. If you want to be important, wonderful. If you want to be great, wonderful. But recognize that he who is greatest among you shall be your servant."

My husband, Martin Luther King, Jr., knew that the true meaning of achievement is service. When I met him, in 1952, he was already ordained as a Baptist preacher and was working toward a doctoral degree at Boston University. I was studying at the New England Conservatory and dreamed of accomplishments in music. We married a year later, and after I graduated the following year we moved to Montgomery, Alabama. We didn't know it then, but our notions of achievement were about to undergo a dramatic change.

You may have read or heard about what happened next. What began with the boycott of a local bus line grew into a national movement, and by the time he was assassinated in 1968 my husband had fashioned a black movement powerful enough to shatter forever the practice of racial segregation. What you may not have read about is where he got his method for resisting injustice without compromising his religious beliefs.

He adopted the strategy of nonviolence from a man of a different race, who lived in a different country, and even practiced a different religion. The man was Mahatma Gandhi, the great leader of India, who devoted his life to serving humanity in the spirit of love and nonviolence. It was in these principles that Martin discovered his method for social reform. More than anything else, those two principles were the key to his achievements.

This book is about black Americans who served society through the excellence of their achievements. It forms a part of the rich history of black men and women in America—a history of stunning accomplishments in every field of human endeavor, from literature and art to science, industry, education, diplomacy, athletics, jurisprudence, even polar exploration.

Not all of the people in this history had the same ideals, but I think you will find something that all of them had in common. Like Martin Luther King, Jr., they all decided to become "drum majors" and serve humanity. In that principle—whether it was expressed in books, inventions, or song—they found something outside themselves to use as a goal and a guide. Something that showed them a way to serve others, instead of only living for themselves.

Reading the stories of these courageous men and women not only helps us discover the principles that we will use to guide our own lives but also teaches us about our black heritage and about America itself. It is crucial for us to know the heroes and heroines of our history and to realize that the price we paid in our struggle for equality in America was dear. But we must also understand that we have gotten as far as we have partly because America's democratic system and ideals made it possible.

We are still struggling with racism and prejudice. But the great men and women in this series are a tribute to the spirit of our democratic ideals and the system in which they have flourished. And that makes their stories special and worth knowing. ◆

1

"TO HELL WITH DYING"

❧

One of the most celebrated authors of our time, Alice Walker blossomed as a writer while attending college in the early 1960s. During her senior year, she drew on her personal experiences to write the short story and poems that eventually became her first published works.

WITH A RAZOR blade clutched in her fingers, 20-year-old Alice Walker paced across her dormitory room. Gray sleet battered the window; the radiator hissed. A thousand miles from her southern home, winter had clamped down in all its gloom.

In Walker's closet hung the few wool skirts and sweaters she had collected during her months in the bitter northern climate, clothes that seemed plain and cheap compared to the designer wear of her wealthy college classmates. On one of the walls hung a newspaper photograph of civil rights leader Martin Luther King, Jr. As a teenager, she had marched behind King in Atlanta, thrilling to his message of racial equality. And just a little more than a year earlier, in August 1963, she had traveled to the nation's capital to attend the civil rights movement's crowning event: the massive March on Washington for Jobs and Freedom, where King ended the daylong rally by delivering his rousing "I Have a Dream" speech.

One month after the March on Washington, Walker had escaped the turmoil of the South for the high-minded serenity of prestigious Sarah Lawrence College, set among the rolling hills of Westchester County in Bronxville, New York. There she had joined a handful of black students in an otherwise

Walker resided in this dormitory while pursuing her bachelor's degree at Sarah Lawrence College in Bronxville, New York. She had transferred there from Spelman College in Atlanta, where, she said, "I wanted to be myself and could not."

all-white environment. But in moving north, had she betrayed her hero?

Every item in Walker's little room stood for a memory, and each one seemed to mock her. On her desk sat the typewriter that had been a gift from her mother years ago, when Alice first left home. The typewriter had been meant to show she could escape the poverty of a sharecropper's life in rural Georgia. Fingers that could type might never have to pick cotton for pennies, as her parents did. Among her seven brothers and sisters, Walker knew she was her mother's fondest hope.

But not now. After completing her first year at Sarah Lawrence, joyful Alice, witty Alice, watchful, gentle Alice had returned from a remarkable journey, one her parents could barely imagine: a summer spent touring tribal villages and wild savannas in Africa, after which she traveled through Europe. Her mind had boggled at all she had seen. The world was a larger, wilder, more generous place than she had dreamed.

Back at school in the fall of 1964, Walker had placed a primitive wooden sculpture from Africa next to her typewriter and hung orange cloth from African markets beside her sweaters. Within weeks, however, all of Walker's excitement had turned to agony. At first, she thought it was a bad cold or the flu. She had never gotten used to the chilly seasons up north. But nausea was not the only sign. By November, she realized that the truth could not be denied any longer: A baby was on the way.

Soon Walker stopped going to classes. "I was so sick," she remembered in *In Search of Our Mother's Gardens: Womanist Prose*, "I could not even bear the smell of fresh air. I lay on my bed in a cold sweat, my head swimming." Night after night she lay awake, unable to rid her mind of one image: the looks that would form on her parents' faces if she had to go home, a few months short of her college degree, with a baby in her arms. They would be crushed to see their last best hope destroyed.

Walker slipped the razor blade under her pillow and slept with it there for a week. Every waking moment became a private debate over whether to slash her wrists with the blade and end her misery, or go on. At one point, she stood at the bathroom sink, tears running down high cheekbones that looked so much like her father's, lightly touching the blade to the pale part of her wrist.

Just then the telephone rang. It was one of the three classmates who knew about Walker's predicament. "I have the phone number of a doctor," the friend said. Walker thanked her and hung up. Then, moving as if in a dream, she made an appointment for an abortion.

"I went to see the doctor," Walker recalled, "and he put me to sleep. When I woke up, my friend was standing over me holding a red rose. She was a blonde, gray-eyed girl, who loved horses and tennis, and she said nothing as she handed me back my life."

Walker's friend drove her back to school and tucked her in bed. Another friend brought Walker food from the cafeteria. Exhausted and emotionally drained, she thanked them and promptly went to sleep.

That night, vivid images of her weeks in Africa filled Walker's dreams: She floated in a boat on a placid lake. Nothing moved; there was no breeze or current. And then, almost magically, there emerged the tiny flicking ears and the broad face of a hippopotamus snorting from the water beside her trailing hand. In another dream, a crocodile emerged from the water. Another time, it was a tiger hiding in the jungle, watching while she ate.

Awaking alone before dawn, Walker nibbled at the sandwiches that had been left for her. Eventually, she picked up a small blue notebook and began to write down her dreams. They came out as short poems, and even though she had rarely written poetry before, the words seemed to pour out of her. Soon each page held a brief, wry observation that read like a verbal snapshot, recalling the scenes in her dreams and then expanding to range over significant memories from her whole life.

The first poem, "African Images, Glimpses from a Tiger's Back," concerned her journey to Africa, expressing wonder at the way unpredictable violence can hide just beneath a veneer of sheer beauty. The 10th stanza of the poem, for example, reads: "The rain forest / Red orchids—glorious! / And near one's eyes / The spinning cobra."

Then, in writing "Karamojans," she thought of her delight at the ironic clash of cultures on the African continent. Walker wrote in the fourth stanza: "A proper English meal / Near the mountains / 'More tea, please' / Down the street / A man walks / Quite completely / Nude."

To tribal princes and to men she had met in Germany, England, and Czechoslovakia, she wrote love poems, such as the one entitled "The Kiss":

i was kissed once
by a beautiful man
all blond and
 czech
riding through bratislava
on a motor bike
screeching "don't yew let me fall off heah naow!"
the funny part was
he spoke english
and setting me gallantly
on my feet
kissed me for
not anyhow *looking*
like aunt jemima.

Before long, Walker began to search further back, remembering images from her youth: her always exhausted father sleeping through a church service, her grandmother spoon-feeding her ailing husband, the spooky fragrance of magnolia blossoms. She also tried to shape into words the numbing anger and frustration she felt over racism in the South, describing horrible lynchings and mutilations in the opening stanza of "South: The Name of Home":

all that night
I prayed for eyes to see again
whose last sight
had been
a broken bottle
held negligently
in a racist
fist
God give us trees to plant
and hands and eyes to
love them.

Even as Walker scribbled in her notebook and gradually grew stronger, the razor blade lay beneath her pillow. Sometimes it took all her strength, it seemed, not to use it. She entitled one poem "Suicide" and another "to die before one wakes must be glad"; yet another poem imagines a suicide caused by the fear of bringing a mixed-race baby home to black parents.

Before dawn every morning, Walker slipped on her boots and donned an overcoat over her nightgown, crept out of her dormitory, and crossed an icy courtyard to the old gardener's cottage in the middle of campus. That was where her adviser, the poet Muriel Rukeyser, held classes. Walker stuffed the poems she had written during the night under the cottage door, then scurried back to her room in the dark. "I didn't care what she did with the poems," Walker said later of Rukeyser, "I only knew I wanted

Jane Cooper (above) was Walker's writing teacher at Sarah Lawrence College; the poet Muriel Rukeyser (opposite page, with Walker) served as her adviser. Together, the two professors offered Walker their support and encouragement and contributed mightily to her development as an author.

someone to read them as if they were new leaves sprouting from an old tree. The same energy that impelled me to write them carried them to her door."

By the end of the week, Walker had used up every page in the notebook, composing an entire collection of poems—a remarkable outburst of creativity by any measure. Yet as she packed her bags to spend the Christmas holidays with one of her friends, she suffered mixed feelings about her poetry. Writing poems had been good therapy, but beyond that what good were they? How did a few pages of words stack up against the gnawing pain she still suffered?

Then a letter arrived from home. A longtime family friend, known as Mr. Sweet, had died. Walker had not thought of the old guitar player in years. During lunchtime at her friend's house, she recounted to her host how the ragged gentleman used to come to her grandmother's kitchen and sit beside the stove, where he would play his beat-up guitar while the solemn old woman busied herself making smothered chicken and biscuits. All of Walker's brothers and sisters would crowd into the room and surround Mr. Sweet while he sang rhymes that referred slyly to events in the community or depicted his times of loneliness and fear. Mr. Sweet could make his guitar sound like a train or a howling dog or a laughing woman, and the plucked strings echoed each word that he sang.

Maybe the old guitarist *had* been a drunk who could not hold down a decent job, but wherever he went in Walker's hometown he won a place of honor at the table. That was because he was an artist, Walker told her friend. "He went deep into his own pain and brought out words and music that made us happy, made us feel empathy for anyone in trouble, made us think," she explained in *Living by the Word*. "We were taught to be thankful that anyone would assume this risk."

Sometimes, it seems, a person has to say something before he or she can believe it. Talking about Mr. Sweet made Walker understand how much she wanted to be an artist, too. That afternoon, she closed the door of the guest room and wrote a short story in honor of old Mr. Sweet. As she recalled years later, "I wrote the story with tears pouring down my cheeks. I was grief-stricken, I was crazed. I was fighting for my own life." As if to end the private debate that had raged within her for weeks, she entitled the story "To Hell with Dying." When she finished the tale, she put the razor blade that she had been keeping under her pillow back in her toilet kit where it belonged.

Walker returned to school in January feeling renewed. Her writing teacher, Jane Cooper, must have sighed with relief to read the new short story,

The poet Langston Hughes was an early champion of Walker's writing and helped publish her first short story, "To Hell with Dying." He described the story to fellow poet Marianne Moore as being written "by the youngest good writer I know, Alice Walker, just past 21."

which so passionately asserted the power of an artist to overcome life's hardest blows. During the fall semester, Walker had turned in only one story, "The Suicide of an American Girl." Reading between the lines, Professor Cooper had feared for Walker's life. Rukeyser had also shown Cooper the poems she had found under her classroom door. Both teachers were thrilled to see how their frightened, unhappy student had turned herself around, producing so much beautiful, telling work in a matter of days.

The two professors talked with Walker, encouraging her to continue writing. "Between them," she remembered later, "they warmly affirmed the life of Mr. Sweet and the vitality of my art, which I was beginning to see merged in unexpected ways, very healing and effective ways, with my life. I was still hanging by a thread, so their enthusiasm was important."

Rukeyser surprised Walker by offering to package her poems and send them to Hiram Haydn, an editor at Harcourt Brace Jovanovich in New York City, who might be willing to publish them in book form. Walker's eyes widened in surprise when Rukeyser added that she had already sent "To Hell with Dying" to the famous poet Langston Hughes. Sure enough, a letter soon arrived from Hughes in which he praised the story and said he would try to publish it! The story came out two years later, just as Hughes had promised. It was Walker's first published work, and it has since been republished, in 1987, as an illustrated children's book.

From Mr. Sweet to Muriel Rukeyser and Jane Cooper on to Langston Hughes, Walker realized that she had been following a chain of mentors all her life. When she finally met Hughes, she was amazed: "He was another Mr. Sweet!" she wrote. "Aging and battered, full of pain, but writing poetry, and laughing, too, and always making other people feel better." For the first time in years, Walker realized that she was not alone. She saw how artists understand that their work is often born of suffering, and they welcome others who can fight through their pain to make a song or a poem or a painting out of it.

Alice Walker could live now. She had found not just a career but a way of life. The written word would sustain her through whatever pain she suffered, it would bring her new friends, and she swore that wherever she went she would share these lessons. Now at the age of 21, she had written a few poems out of her own experience and a couple of short stories that celebrated the lives of people she had known. From such a rich heritage she was sure new creations would come. ◖◗

2

THE NAME OF HOME

ALICE WALKER HAS written that "no one could wish for a more advantageous heritage than that bequeathed to the black writer in the South." At first glance, however, her claim might seem unlikely, for Walker was born into a world of hardship and poverty. The eighth and last child of Willie Lee Walker and the former Minnie Tallulah Grant, she was born Alice Malsenior Walker on February 9, 1944, in Eatonton, Georgia, which she later described as "a town of two streets."

Alice's parents were sharecroppers who earned as little as $300 a year working the farm of an old white woman named Meys, who seemed to own all the land for miles around, including the tiny house into which all the Walkers crowded. The rest of the family—brothers Curtis, Fred, James, Robert, and William; and sisters Molly and Ruth—worked in the fields, too, and Alice's brothers helped their father milk a large herd of cows every morning and afternoon. Willie Lee Walker never took a vacation in his life.

The women seemed to work harder still. Before going to the fields every morning, Minnie Walker, whom Alice described in *In Search of Our Mother's Gardens* as "a large, soft, loving-eyed woman," fed and dressed her growing brood, tidied the house, and

A view of Eatonton, the Georgia town where Walker grew up. "During childhood," she said, "I wasn't aware that there was segregation or that it was designed to make me feel bad. White people just seemed very alien and strange to me."

somehow found time to tend her flower garden, where 50 different kinds of flowers thrived. She showed her daughters how to sew beautiful quilts from scraps of cloth, made all of the children's clothes, and, during the summer harvest, canned vegetables and berries in a hot kitchen.

In this hive of industry, Alice could not help but feel that her birth "elicited more anxiety than joy. It hurt me to think," she recalled in *Living by the Word*, "that for both my parents, poor people, my arrival represented many more years of back-breaking and spirit-crushing toil." But if that was the case, Alice's parents never let on. They doted on their new baby, dressing her in ribbons and petticoats to show her off at church or the county fair. On weekdays, she went with her parents to the fields and played among the morning glory vines while they planted, weeded, and picked their crops.

When Alice turned four, her mother could no longer take her to the fields each day, so Minnie Walker asked Mrs. Reynolds, the local first-grade teacher, if the child could start school at such an early age. Reynolds knew how much store the Walkers put in getting an education. Alice's father had been one of the leading forces years earlier in getting the county's first black school built; her mother was widely known in the community for fighting with her landlord to keep the children in school and out of the fields. So Reynolds agreed.

She made her youngest student feel right at home, too. Together they carved ducks from soap, and as the girl pressed her tiny hand on a sheet of paper, the teacher traced the surprising shape of a chicken around her fingers. Alice Walker said years later of Reynolds: "She taught me that school is a wonderful place, full of people who care about you and your family, and understand you and your ways, and love you for what you are." Such nurturing caused Alice to blossom like one of her mother's flowers. Almost instantly, she proved herself one of the school's brightest students.

It must have been heartbreaking, then, to discover at the age of eight that she would no longer be able to attend the school where Reynolds taught. The Walkers moved to a farm in a neighboring county and enrolled their children in the local school. But during that summer of 1952, before classes started, a greater tragedy struck.

Alice and her brothers loved to play cowboys and Indians, racing about their yard on broomstick horses while acting out the frontier adventures of film heroes Tom Mix and Hopalong Cassidy, whom the children had seen on the movie screen in town. All went well until her brothers received BB guns for their birthdays. After that, Alice was asked to play an Indian all the time, wielding her homemade bow and arrows against their shiny new air rifles. She took the role to heart, creeping from tree to tree or climbing stealthily onto the roof of the makeshift garage to surprise them with a terrifying war whoop.

One day, as she stood atop the garage, holding her bow and arrow and staring out across the broad fields, Alice felt what she later described as an "incredible blow" to her right eye. She looked down just in time to see one of her brothers lower his BB gun. Frightened, the boys helped Alice to the house, all the while trying to make up a story that would keep them out of trouble.

Lying in her mother's arms on the porch, Alice saw the tall tree that grew near the porch, its broad limbs climbing past the railing to the roof. And then, as she has never forgotten, "its leaves [were] blotted out by the rising blood." It was the last thing her right eye ever saw.

Her father tried a home remedy, pressing cool lily leaves on Alice's eye, because he could not afford a

Alice poses for a family snapshot with her mother, Minnie (who is holding a photograph of herself and her husband, Willie Lee). According to Alice, "I grew up believing that there was nothing, literally nothing, my mother couldn't do once she set her mind to it."

One of the more unusual landmarks around Eatonton was Rock Eagle, which the local Cherokee Indians had formed by piling stones onto a mound of earth. Walker took special pride in this monument because she was of Cherokee ancestry.

car and thus had no way of getting his youngest daughter to a doctor's office. A week passed before a physician examined her. By then, "a glob of whitish scar tissue, a hideous cataract," Alice later called it, had formed on her eye. She could not bear to look at herself in the mirror or raise her head to look at anyone else.

Then, to make matters worse, classes started. Her new school was a cold and drafty stone building that had once been the state penitentiary. To scare each other, students climbed to a tiny room on the third floor and dared one another to peek at the shadowy outline where an electric chair had sat. Alice hated the place. Her brothers were constantly getting into fights to stop the other students from teasing her about her injured eye. For the first time, her grades suffered.

It did not take long for Minnie Walker to take action. She sent Alice to live with her grandparents in Eatonton so she could attend her old school. There Alice's grades improved, but she still felt like a freak. She walked with her head bent down and spent all her free time reading or scribbling in a notebook.

Her parents did what they could to draw her out. When Alice came home on weekends, they sat

around the fireplace telling wondrous stories that
made her forget herself for a while. Alice's father told
about his great-great-great grandmother Mary Poole,
a slave who was forced to walk from Virginia to
Georgia, hauling a baby on each hip. ("She really was
a *Walker*," he would joke.) Alice's mother told of
her grandmother Tallulah, a stern-faced old woman
who was mostly Cherokee Indian. Minnie Walker made Alice understand that the nearby Indian
mound known as Rock Eagle, made of stones piled
eight feet high in the shape of an eagle, had been
built by the Cherokee and was a part of Alice's
heritage.

There were other stories, too, of mythical characters named Tar Baby and Brer Rabbit, funny stories
that had been passed down in the family for genera-
tions. When Alice grew up, she learned that these
tales could be traced all the way back to Africa and
to Native American tribes.

Alice was also able to relax and forget about her
injured eye while in church. At Sunday homecoming
picnics and barbecues, the church women would slip
her a dime or a nickel, pinch her cheek, and predict
a wonderful future for her. She loved the way people
shared everything from baby clothes to funeral expenses. "Depending on one another, because they had
nothing and no one else, the sharecroppers often
managed to come through 'all right,'" she wrote in *In
Search of Our Mother's Gardens*. "Because we never
believed we were poor, and therefore worthless,
we could depend on one another without shame."
Alice carried that sense of community as her shield
wherever she went.

Gradually, however, she watched the community
break apart. Wanting to make more money than they
could as farmhands, her brothers left home one by
one and moved a thousand miles away, to Boston,
Massachusetts. Her sisters made similar plans.

Walker was baptized at Ward's Chapel in Eatonton and faithfully attended the religious services held in the church. Equally important to her personal development were the people she met there.

Worst of all, Alice watched as the fat and jolly man who was her father shrank under the burden of hard work, low pay, and too many cigarettes, growing thin and leathery, coughing as he came up the stairs, fighting diabetes and emphysema. To earn a bit more money, her mother stopped laboring in the fields and worked as a maid for a white woman in town. In what little spare time she had, Minnie Walker continued to grow flowers, creating a gorgeous blossoming garden around their modest home.

Alice was 14 years old when she finally got the chance to visit her favorite brother, Bill, up north. During the visit, he talked her into going to a hospital for an eye operation. Afterward, the doctor told Alice that he could not save the vision in her right eye, but that did not matter so much. She was overjoyed to see that the ugly white glob on her eye had been removed. All that was left was a "small bluish crater" where the scar tissue had been.

Alice returned to Eatonton renewed. She wasted no time in winning the boyfriend she had dreamed about since she was 6, a 15-year-old with "deep-brown skin and laughing hazel eyes," Taylor Reese. All through high school they dated every Saturday night without fail. Alice thought of him as her best friend. He was "loyal, gentle, thoughtful, loving.

Good," she wrote years later. In his arms, she began to feel beautiful for the first time. And when the student body showed it agreed, electing her prom queen in her senior year, Reese walked beside Alice as her proud escort.

From time to time, people would ask Alice what she wanted to do with her life. Would she follow her eldest sister, Molly, whom Alice later described as "a brilliant, studious girl who became one of those Negro wonders—who collected scholarships like trading stamps and wandered all over the world"? Would she follow her brothers to Boston? Or would she wait a while before testing her wings, working in town as her sister Ruth did, as a hairdresser?

Alice looked about Eatonton with wistful eyes. A bright student would be mad, it seemed, to stay. In Eatonton, blacks were not even allowed to sit at the drugstore lunch counter or use the rest rooms at the bus station, much less hope for a good job. But she loved her friends, her mother's garden, the ladies at church, her teachers, the old guitarist Mr. Sweet. The stories she had heard made her feel rooted to the land, even if she did not own it.

For months Alice pondered her problem. Then, on Wednesday, October 19, 1960, as she watched a soap opera on the beat-up black-and-white television her mother had brought home, the answer came. A news bulletin cut into the program, showing the minister of a black church in nearby Atlanta, dressed in a sharply creased suit and thin-brimmed hat, being pushed roughly into the back of a police van. The camera focused on hundreds of people surrounding the van, touching its sides, and singing "We Shall Overcome," as if they were not afraid of the police. The announcer said the minister's name was Martin Luther King, Jr. The people had been picketing a department store because its lunch counter was off-limits to blacks.

Civil rights leader Martin Luther King, Jr., first came into Walker's life on an autumn afternoon in 1960, when a television news bulletin showed him being arrested at a nonviolent demonstration in Atlanta. The scene inspired Walker to take an active role in the civil rights movement.

In that moment, the civil rights movement entered Alice Walker's life. "Dr. Martin Luther King, Jr. was the first black face I saw on our new television screen," she recalled. "As in a fairy tale, my soul was stirred by the meaning for me of his mission. I saw in him the hero for whom I had waited so long."

Walker found the bulletin much more gripping than any soap opera. Here was a man daring to ask why black patrons were not allowed to sit beside whites and order a soft drink or a sandwich. And the people standing around the police van, singing "We Shall Overcome," seemed just like him. They were taking a stand on home turf, demanding justice where they lived.

In an instant, Walker's problem about what she should do after graduation had been solved. She vowed to join the protesters, using all her youthful energy to make her home a place from which no one would need to escape. On the spot, she decided to go to Atlanta after high school and take part in the civil rights movement. That night, her mother, also clearly moved by what she had seen on television, added King's name to the list of people for whom she prayed.

Walker graduated from high school in the spring of 1961. Her parents vied with Taylor Reese for applauding the loudest at the ceremony, as Walker was honored as class valedictorian. Almost as reward-ing, she had been voted by the other seniors as the most popular girl in the school. Formerly painfully shy and self-conscious, she had turned her life around after her traumatic accident by taking the time, she said later, "really to see people and things, really to notice relationships and to learn to be patient enough to care about how they turned out."

One other positive thing emerged from the eye injury: It enabled Walker to apply for a scholarship for handicapped students to Atlanta University's prestigious Spelman College, the best black women's college in the nation. When Walker received word that she had won the scholarship, she knew for sure that she no longer had to worry about what to do after school. Her immediate future was set.

It was not lost on Walker that Atlanta University was located in the heart of the burgeoning civil rights movement. Just weeks prior to her high school graduation, students in Atlanta had organized an enormous protest rally. Nearly 1,500 picketers had encircled the entire downtown area, demanding equal treatment for blacks and whites.

Seventeen-year-old Alice Walker looked forward to increasing their number. The flickering image of Martin Luther King, Jr., on a television screen had lit the way. Now she wanted nothing more than to join King and his followers, live on the streets of Atlanta. ❧

3

"THE NATURE OF THIS FLOWER IS TO BLOOM"

As ALICE WALKER packed to leave for Spelman College in August 1961, she heard a knock on the front door. When she went to answer it, a neighbor greeted her, then thrust $75 into the teenager's hands and said the money had been raised to cover her bus fare to Atlanta. One of Walker's sisters had already given her a check for $300 to pay for living expenses. And somehow, despite her salary of only $20 a week, Alice's mother had managed to buy her 17-year-old daughter a suitcase, a sewing machine, and a typewriter. There was a special reason, Minnie Walker told Alice, why she had chosen each of the gifts. The suitcase was for independence, the sewing machine for self-sufficiency, and the typewriter for creativity.

Walker (far right) flanks some of her classmates at Spelman College. She later said of the two years she spent at the school: "I wanted to be myself and I could not do that while thinking about whether my seams were straight, and my hair was straight, and my dress was ironed, and my slip wasn't showing. The administration made it clear that if we were arrested in political demonstrations, we could be expelled."

Her father said nothing during Alice's leave-taking. Willie Lee Walker helped his youngest daughter load her baggage into the luggage compartment of a Greyhound bus, then watched as she boarded it alone. When the bus pulled away, she turned in her seat to see him standing in the road, watching silently, a gray fedora in his hands.

Years later, after her father had died, Walker would dream of this scene again and wake up crying. But now she squared her shoulders and prepared for the challenge that lay ahead in Atlanta. Then she thought, Why wait? Choosing that moment to commit her first overt political act, she moved to the front of the bus, which was reserved for whites only, and took a seat.

Immediately, a white woman complained to the driver. And just as quickly, the driver—"big and red and ugly," Walker recalled—ordered her to move. "I moved," she wrote later, "but in those seconds of moving, everything changed. I was eager to bring an end to the South that permitted my humiliation."

Walker arrived in Atlanta just as the leadership of the Student Nonviolent Coordinating Committee (SNCC), an organization that coordinated student-led civil rights activities in the South, began attempting to desegregate public facilities in Albany, a city of nearly 60,000 in southern Georgia. One year earlier, SNCC had held sit-ins at Rich's, a downtown Atlanta department store, demanding that blacks be allowed to dine at the same lunch counters as whites. The demonstrations had proven successful, and the SNCC leaders had sworn to continue their campaign until "every vestige of racial segregation and discrimination is erased from the face of the earth."

It must have been difficult for Walker to keep her mind on schoolwork with so much heroism in the air. Nevertheless, she worked hard at her studies, falling in love with the Russian writers of the 19th century—especially Fyodor Dostoyevsky, Nikolay Gogol, Maksim Gorky, Ivan Turgenev, and, above all, Lev Tolstoy—reading them "as if they were a delicious cake." She appreciated how each author rooted his soul in the soil of his native land, and she would remember this practice well. Walker also admired the way Tolstoy's stories always dug past politics, to get at "the essential spirit of individual persons." When she began to write stories, she tried to live up to his example.

As much as Walker loved her schoolwork, she did not find it easy to get along with her classmates. Describing her college days in the novel *Meridian*, she wrote: "Most of the students—timid, imitative, bright enough but never daring, were being ushered nearer to Ladyhood every day. It was for this that their parents had sent them to [Spelman] College. They learned to make French food, English tea and German music without once having the urge to slip off the heavily guarded campus." In addition to the school's strict curfews, there was a saying at Spelman that "you could do anything there as long as you wore white gloves"; it meant, of course, that a young woman who kept her gloves clean could not do anything interesting. Walker chafed at such restrictions.

At the end of her freshman year, she was rewarded for her hard work with the opportunity to make her first trip to Europe. A group of Atlanta churchwomen offered to sponsor her as a delegate to the World Youth Peace Festival in Helsinki, Finland. Walker happily agreed to attend the two-week conference; before leaving, however, she and a fellow delegate shared in an even greater honor: They were invited into the home of their hero, Martin Luther King, Jr., for a chat with his wife, Coretta.

The visit to the Kings' house made for an afternoon that Walker has never forgotten. In the

Parents and children in Albany, Georgia, join forces for a civil rights march in July 1962. When Walker returned to Spelman College that autumn to begin her sophomore year, she discovered that her classmates, inspired by the Albany protests, were eager to join the ranks of the demonstrators.

"modest, bare looking house with exceedingly non-descript furniture," Coretta Scott King warmly greeted the two students. "Coretta that day was quick, bright-eyed, slim, and actually bubbly," Walker recalled, "and very girlish-looking with her face free of make-up, shining a little, and her long hair tied in a simple, slightly curly, ponytail." As the women discussed the worldwide civil rights movement for a while, Walker could barely contain her excitement. She was convinced that somewhere in the little house, even though he never showed himself, King was busy working.

A continent away, Walker again had cause to be wide eyed. At the World Youth Peace Festival, she witnessed "spectacular cultural programs, mass political rallies, and countless seminars on the struggle in Africa, Latin America, Asia, the Middle East." Caught up in the spirit of the festival, she leaped to join an exuberant conga line led by the Cuban delegation, and they all poured into the icy Finnish streets, with everyone laughing and singing of freedom. Apparently, Walker's full schedule in Helsinki did not permit her to meet another American delegate at the conference, the budding black militant Angela Davis.

When the World Youth Peace Festival ended, Walker and some other delegates traveled by train to the Soviet Union. At this point in her life, she knew so little about world history that upon visiting Red Square in Moscow, Walker admitted later, she "could not fathom for the longest time *who* the Russians were queuing up to view in Lenin's tomb." From the stately gray streets of Leningrad she brought back only the memory of a vibrant little girl with orange and yellow flowers clutched tightly in her hand.

Walker remained in Europe through the summer of 1962. Meanwhile, student activists were still pushing ahead with their attempt to desegregate the South. Half a year earlier, SNCC had successfully mobilized the entire black community in Albany, with a large number of demonstrators getting thrown in jail for taking part in the protests. According to William G. Anderson, leader of the Albany Movement, "There was a change in attitude of the kids who saw their parents step into the forefront and lead the demonstrations. They were determined that they would never go through what their parents went through to get the recognition that they should have as citizens." Walker returned to school to find Spelman students, in their starched white dresses and white gloves, proudly joining picket lines and going to jail for the rights they demanded.

Walker was ready to join them. "During my sophomore year," she wrote, "I stood on the grass in front of Trevor-Arnett Library at Atlanta University and I listened to the young leaders of SNCC. John Lewis was there, and so was Julian Bond (thin, well-starched and ironed in light-colored jeans); he looked (with his cropped hair that still tried to curl) like a poet (which he was). Everyone was beautiful, because everyone was conquering fear by holding the hands of the persons next to them."

Walker joined the student protesters as they endured taunts at lunch counter sit-ins. She also picketed churches, department stores, and jails. Scenes of cowardly violence by white racists and of steely determination by the nonviolent black and white protesters during these demonstrations have since found expression in her stories, poems, and essays. She recalled in *Meridian*, for example: "[I] saw small black children, with short, flashing black legs, being chased by grown white men brandishing axe handles. [I] saw old women dragged out of stores and beaten on the sidewalk, their humility of a lifetime doing them no good."

By the end of Walker's sophomore year, the tension between Spelman's efforts to make her into a proper young women and the constant danger she faced at the civil rights demonstrations had exhausted her completely. Needing a break from schoolwork and picketing, she decided to spend the summer with her brother Bill in Boston, where she took a part-time job and earned a bit of money for the coming school year.

Near the end of August, Walker left New England and, traveling alone by bus, returned to the Deep South by way of Washington, D.C. There, on August 28, 1963, she joined the nearly 250,000 people who participated in a massive demonstration in the nation's capital: the March on Washington for Jobs

Walker said of the March on Washington for Jobs and Freedom, the massive civil rights demonstration that was held in the nation's capital on August 28, 1963, "I wouldn't have missed it for the world. It was one of those days when you feel the tide is turning and you are with the tide. I heard every word, and every word went through my whole body and through my whole soul."

and Freedom. The protesters gathered at the Washington Monument and proceeded to the Lincoln Memorial, where a huge rally was held.

Walker could not get anywhere near the rostrum at the Lincoln Memorial as speaker after speaker addressed the crowd. "I was perched on the limb of a tree far from the Lincoln Memorial," she recalled, "and although I managed to see very little of the speakers, I could hear everything." Martin Luther King, Jr., was the last speaker of the day, and he delivered the inspiring address for which he is best remembered, stirring his listeners with the ringing phrase, "I have a dream."

An exhilarated Walker returned to Spelman that September, eager to continue her work with SNCC.

She again ran up against the stiff curfews of the school administrators, however, and before long it seemed that she had two enemies: the university, which wanted her to become a lady, and what she called "the larger, more deadly enemy, white racist society." Walker had already seen classmates collapse with the tension of juggling so many demands, and she did not wish to join them in the infirmary.

When prestigious Sarah Lawrence College offered Walker a scholarship, she did not know what to do. Fortunately, her favorite teachers, Staughton Lynd and Howard Zinn, saw both sides of the issue. Although they wanted Walker to continue her studies at Spelman, they realized that her proximity to the civil rights movement might drag her away from college altogether. Sarah Lawrence, on the other hand, was an excellent school, out of the line of fire.

With her teachers assuring her that there would be plenty of work to undertake in the civil rights movement after she received a college degree, Walker decided to accept the scholarship and the novelty of studying at a mostly white college. She packed her warmest clothes and caught the train to New York after Christmas. Her "only regret," she recalled later, "was that I would miss the Saturday morning demonstrations downtown that had become indispensable to education in the Atlanta University Center."

Sarah Lawrence College took some getting used to, though. For one thing, Walker remembered, "there were only three or four other black people there, and no poor people at all as far as the eye could see." Despite being out of her element, she found exactly what she had been looking for: "Freedom to come and go, to read leisurely, to go my own way, dress my own way, and conduct my personal life as I saw fit."

Walker soon added a whole shelf full of library books to the Russian novels she loved so much: volumes by the Japanese haiku masters Bashō and Shiki, the 8th-century Chinese poet Li Po, and the American poets e. e. cummings, Emily Dickinson, and William Carlos Williams. Of the period in which she discovered their work, she said: "My feet did not touch the ground."

Walker studied literature at Sarah Lawrence with Jane Cooper and Muriel Rukeyser, although it was not until her senior year that she began to take her own writing seriously. Reeling from an eye-opening tour of Africa and recovering from the pain of pregnancy and an abortion, she poured out her thoughts in telling phrases that surprised and gratified her teachers. They encouraged her to keep writing and promised to introduce her to influential editors in New York City. Walker thrilled to her professors' attention, and when she graduated from Sarah Lawrence in 1965, she promised them she would write a poem, a story—something—every day.

Walker, however, had not forgotten her commitment to the civil rights movement. With the passage of the Civil Rights Act of 1964, a swift blow had been dealt to racial discrimination in the South. The law banned segregation in public accommodations; unions and employers were forbidden to practice racial discrimination; and institutions that discriminated against blacks were denied federal funds. Yet racial discrimination still occurred at polling places across the Deep South, where white local officials employed a variety of means to prevent blacks from registering to vote.

In response, civil rights activists traveled door-to-door across the South, encouraging blacks to register. Wary of the danger involved in rankling white authorities but determined to reach even those homes

President Lyndon B. Johnson signs the Voting Rights Act of 1965, which protected black voters against disfranchisement. By working as a voter registration volunteer, Walker and thousands of other civil rights activists prompted the federal government to pass the bill into law.

set far off the main roads, Walker worked in the swampy coastal area of Liberty County, Georgia. She spent her time, she recalled, "helping to canvass voters and in general looking at the South to see if it was worth claiming."

In "You Can't Keep a Good Woman Down," a short story written 10 years later, Walker described a typical day working with a partner, the white Luna, as a voter registration volunteer: "She walked ten miles a day with me up and down those straight Georgia highways, stopping at every house that looked black (you could always tell in those days) and asking whether anyone needed help with learning how to vote. The simple mechanics: writing one's name, or making one's 'X' in the proper column. And then, though we were required to walk, everywhere, we were empowered to offer prospective registrants a car in which they might safely ride down to the county courthouse. And later to the polling places."

In time, the efforts of Walker and the other activists would prompt the federal government to address the problem of black disfranchisement. The Voting Rights Act of 1965 would provide for federal registrars to make sure that the rights of black voters were not being denied.

During the period that Walker worked as a voter registration volunteer, she visited her parents in Eatonton and was saddened to see how they had changed since she had left home. Her father "was visibly ill, paranoid, complaining the whole time of [her] mother's religious activities." Her mother, with the kids out of the house, had become a Jehovah's Witness, praying and recruiting new members with all of her considerable strength.

Walker left Georgia that fall for New York City, where she took an apartment in the poverty-ridden Lower East Side, on St. Marks Place, a street famed for its beatniks and folksingers. The apartment building did not even have a front door, and roaches scattered whenever she turned on the lights. With cheerful determination, she set up a writing desk near the window and found a job in the city's welfare department.

To her great delight, Walker soon won a writing fellowship from the Bread Loaf Writer's Conference. When the first check arrived, she considered leaving her grimy neighborhood to move to Senegal in West Africa, a country she remembered fondly from her visit there the previous summer. But the civil rights movement continued to beckon, and in the summer of 1966, Walker decided to face the ugly contradictions of the American South head on. She promptly caught a plane for Jackson, Mississippi, the very heart of Dixie.

Two of the more shockingly violent episodes in the civil rights movement had already occurred in Mississippi. In June 1963, a gunman had killed Medgar Evers, a prominent civil rights leader, in front of his Jackson home. One year later, an interracial team of three civil rights workers—James Chaney, Andrew Goodman, and Michael Schwerner—had disappeared mysteriously; their bodies were later found near the small town of Philadelphia in central Mississippi.

Walker has explained her courageous decision to settle in Mississippi in *In Search of Our Mother's Gardens*: "That summer marked the beginning of a realization that I could never live happily in Africa—or anywhere else—until I could live freely in Mississippi." Like the defiant SNCC volunteers in Georgia, she refused to be run out of her native land. She wrote in her journal that she wanted to "tirelessly observe" the South, "to kill the fear it engendered in my imagination as a place where black life was terrifyingly hard, pitifully cheap."

Once again, Walker volunteered to go door-to-door in the poorest counties of the nation's poorest state, helping people fill out voter registration cards. It was hard work but gratifying in many ways. Walker was moved by the stubborn ingenuity with which country people faced poverty. Every door that opened to her knock revealed a dramatic story. She swore that she would write them all down as soon as the chance came.

Then, almost on first sight, she fell in love with a fellow volunteer, whom she later described as "a soulful young Jewish law student named Mel Leventhal." He was, she said, "warm, openly and spontaneously affectionate," and he enjoyed talking with her about anything and everything. He also seemed genuinely interested in her writing and encouraged her to keep at it.

Filled with idealism, Leventhal planned to use his law degree to battle racial discrimination in the courtroom; Walker liked the sound of that. Though it was dangerous for an interracial couple to walk hand in hand in rural Mississippi, the two found private moments for talking, swimming, and feasting on fried chicken. When their summer of canvassing and kissing ended, Leventhal flew north to return to New York University Law School. Alice Walker sat beside him on the plane. ❧

4

IN LOVE
AND TROUBLE

Walker at work on her first novel, The Third Life of Grange Copeland. *It took her two years to complete the manuscript, which was published in 1970.*

M EL LEVENTHAL WOOED Alice Walker with two things no poet could resist: genuine respect for her writing, and flowers.

Back in her "dank, poorly-lighted" apartment on St. Marks Place, Walker had made plans to begin work on a novel. More and more, however, she found herself at Leventhal's small yet cheerful apartment overlooking Washington Square Park. To make the place more appealing, Leventhal brought a metal folding table from his mother's house in Brooklyn, set it beside the tall double windows, and covered it with a madras bedspread. Walker placed a brown earthenware vase—a gift from a college friend—on the table; from then on, she recalled, Leventhal made sure the vase "was always full of white daisies or, in the spring, pink peonies."

Leventhal invited Walker to make the table her writing desk. She soon lugged her typewriter over, placed it beside the vase, and began to work on her novel, while he studied across the park at the New

York University library. Trees and grass stretched before her; the gentle scent of cut flowers suggested the gardens of her youth. Gradually, she was able to blot out the city's car horns and sirens and imagine the rural world her fictional characters inhabited.

When winter came, however, the bare trees seemed to offer nothing but spindly backdrops for gritty snow. Walker set her novel aside and began work on an essay entitled "The Civil Rights Movement: What Good Was It?" In it, she recounted her discovery of Martin Luther King, Jr., SNCC, sit-ins, and marches. Because of them, she wrote, "I have fought harder for my life and for a chance to be myself, to be something more than a shadow or a number."

The civil rights movement, Walker concluded in the essay, "gave us history and men far greater than Presidents. It gave us heroes, selfless men of courage and strength, for our little boys and girls to follow. It gave us hope for tomorrow. It called us to life. Because we live, it can never die."

"The Civil Rights Movement: What Good Was It?" became Walker's first published essay and in 1967 won the $300 first prize in the annual *American Scholar* magazine essay contest. The money "was almost magically reassuring," she wrote later, "during those days of disaffected parents, outraged friends, and one-item meals, and kept us in tulips, peonies, daisies, and lamb chops for several months."

Having decided that she needed to be in the country to write about country folk, Walker applied for a writing fellowship to the MacDowell Colony in Peterborough, New Hampshire. She was awarded a fellowship and moved to New England after Christmas to work among other writers and artists in the colony's truly rural environment. Surrounded by snowswept fir trees in a cabin warmed by a crackling fire, and playing gospel records by Clara Ward and

Walker's literary career received a significant boost in 1967, when the MacDowell Colony in Peterborough, New Hampshire, awarded her this cabin, known as the Irving Fine Studio, in which to work on The Third Life of Grange Copeland. *She found the solitude of the writer's colony so beneficial to her concentration that she later returned there to complete another project.*

Mahalia Jackson as she typed, Walker made great progress on her novel, finishing six chapters in as many weeks.

Leventhal arrived every weekend in his red Volkswagen Beetle, the backseat, Walker recalled, "stuffed to the windows with flowers, grapefruit and oranges." He proposed marriage during one of these visits, and a short time later the two lovers packed the Volkswagen with her belongings, said goodbye to the MacDowell Colony (although she returned there again in 1977, when she was awarded another fellowship), and drove back to New York. There, on March 17, 1967, Leventhal and the 23-year-old Walker were wed. True to his word, Leventhal made plans to join the battle for civil rights in Mississippi after he graduated from law school in May. "We could challenge the laws against intermarriage at the same time," Walker observed. "Love, politics, work—it was a mighty coming together." Friends predicted that life would not be easy for an interracial couple—both of them social activists—setting up house in the heart of Dixie, and they were not mistaken.

When the newlyweds arrived in the state capital of Jackson, they became the first legally married interracial couple to reside in the city. Walker has since written, "I felt then—as I do now—that in order to be able to live at all in America I must be unafraid to live anywhere in it, and I must be able to live in the fashion and with whom I choose."

Walker and Leventhal moved into an old home on Rockdale Street and made friends easily with their neighbors. But the newlyweds could not ignore the constant threats and taunts that faced them else-where. They soon learned that even going to the movies together might cause a race riot. Over the next several years, Walker and Leventhal lived in a state of constant vigilance and worry. Sometimes they felt as if they were wearing bull's-eyes on their backs. For safety's sake, they bought a watchdog and a rifle.

But the threat of violence did not keep them from fulfilling their mission. Leventhal, working closely with the local chapter of the National Association for the Advancement of Colored People (NAACP), filed suits against restaurants that would not seat black patrons, against hotels that restricted blacks from using the swimming pools, and against any business in town that denied equal treatment to all. Meanwhile, Walker went to work as a teacher.

First, she became a black history consultant to preschool teachers at the Friends of the Children of Mississippi, part of the federal government's newly formed Head Start program, which provides meals, health care, and preschool education to un-derprivileged children. Working closely with the teachers, many of whom possessed only a fifth-grade education and had little enthusiasm for history, Walker succeeded in interesting them in the subject by asking them to write their autobiographies. At first, these churchgoing country women needed to be prodded into exploring the difficult issues in their lives. But before the classes ended—a casualty of budget cutbacks—many of the teachers had turned in lucid, moving accounts of their struggles. Walker arranged for all the stories to be copied and stapled together, then handed them back to her students as a sort of patchwork quilt in words. Comparing the tales, she hoped, would help them understand the larger currents of politics and habit that they shared—in short, the importance of history. An unexpected bonus was that she found herself all but overwhelmed with material to write about. She has said that she found "the stories knee-deep" in Mississippi, adding that her time there "was a period of constant revelation, when mysteries not understood during my Southern childhood came naked to me to be embraced. I grew to adulthood in Mississippi."

Poems soon filled the pages of Walker's notebooks. The gestures of wizened old women found their way into her short stories. Her daily immersion in the troubles of her neighbors and students also sharpened the childhood memories from which her novel was being drawn.

By early 1968, Walker was expecting a baby. She wondered aloud how it would be possible to raise a child, hold down a job, and continue to write. But she realized that an unexpected benefit of motherhood might be that it would keep her husband out of the army. The deployment of thousands of American combat troops in Southeast Asia had expanded into a full-fledged war in Vietnam—a war the pacifistic couple staunchly opposed. Leventhal would not have to enter the army, however, if the military draft board deemed him a "family man."

In the midst of preparing room for a baby in her busy life, Walker received some crushing news. She was watching television on April 4, 1968, when it was announced that Martin Luther King, Jr., had been assassinated in Memphis, Tennessee. "It was," Walker recalled, "as if the last light in my world had gone out."

The first black woman to receive a Guggenheim Fellowship, Nella Larsen wrote two novels, Quicksand *(1928) and* Passing *(1929), during the black cultural movement known as the Harlem Renaissance. Nearly half a century later, Walker discovered Larsen's writings and launched a campaign to promote her work as well as that of other long-forgotten black authors.*

A mule-drawn caisson carries
the coffin of Martin Luther King,
Jr., through the streets of Atlanta
on April 9, 1968. The civil
rights leader's assassination made
Walker feel, she said, "as if
the last light in my world had
gone out."

That weekend, she and her husband flew to
Atlanta, King's hometown, to attend the funeral. As
the mule-drawn wagon bearing King's coffin made its
way through the city's streets, Walker and her husband marched behind it, accompanied by nearly
100,000 other mourners. Along the route stood a
number of landmarks that served as testimony to the
slain civil rights leader: the department stores, bus
stations, churches, and jails where some of the key
battles in the civil rights movement had been fought
and won.

It was all too much for Walker. In an essay written
three years later, she remembered: "The week after
that long, four-mile walk across Atlanta, and after
the tears and anger and the feeling of turning gradually to stone, I lost the child I had been carrying. I did
not even care. It seemed to me, at the time, that if

'he' (it was weeks before my tongue could form his name) must die no one deserved to live, not even my own child."

Thoughts of suicide, which had not tormented Walker since her days at Sarah Lawrence College, crept back to haunt her. Around this time, the poetry she had written during her darkest days in college was published as *Once*. But not even the sight of her very first book offered Walker much consolation. Neither did teaching black studies at Jackson State University, where she held a writer-in-residence position from 1968 to 1969, nor winning a National Endowment for the Arts grant in 1969. She tried to combat her depression with hard work, and sometimes she succeeded. But her bad days were filled with rage and tears.

In March 1969, Walker discovered that she was expecting again. It was not a smooth pregnancy. "The first three months I vomited," she remembered. "The middle three I felt fine and flew off to look at ruins in Mexico. The last three I was so big at 170 pounds I looked like someone else, which did not please me." Walker's only real pleasure during this period came in grappling with the characters of her novel. For two years, she had worked on the tale, completely rewriting the version she had drafted in the North. In November 1969, with the baby due any day, she finished the last page.

Harcourt Brace Jovanovich published Walker's novel the following year. Entitled *The Third Life of Grange Copeland*, it is built around a horrifying experience that happened while she was in high school: the shotgun murder of a neighbor, also named Walker, by the woman's husband. Alice's sister Ruth was working at the time as a hairdresser and cosmetician and was sometimes asked to beautify corpses at the nearby funeral home. One night, Ruth asked Alice to accompany her on the particularly frightening assignment of dressing the hair of the murdered Walker woman. The two held hands in fear as they stepped into the mortuary to do what they could to make their neighbor appear presentable. The murdered woman's body lay on the table, her face entirely blown off by the force of the shotgun blast.

Walker began to wonder how a man could do that to his own wife, even someone known to be as mean and abusive as the woman's murderous husband. What had happened to their love? And what made women put up with such brutality?

The Third Life of Grange Copeland is Walker's exploration of those and other questions. In writing the novel, she imagined the life of the murdered Walker woman, trying to chart the course of her neighbor's tragic marriage through the characters of the southern tenant farmer Brownsfield Copeland and his wife, Mem. In doing so, Walker brought to bear all her experience as a daughter of sharecroppers and as a careful observer of poverty and hardship.

In the relationship of Brownsfield and Mem Copeland, Walker exposed the system of sharecropping, indicting it for beating people down so cruelly that some of them are driven to brutalize their loved ones. It is a gripping tale, riveting in its relentless description of a family's headlong destruction. And it comes to a horrifying climax with the shotgun murder of the long-suffering Mem.

In the second half of the novel, Walker attempted to dig the reader out of that pit of hatred and despair. When Copeland is sent to prison, his long-absent father, Grange, who had deserted his family for a chance to live in the North, resurfaces to take custody of Brownsfield's daughter, Ruth, and raise her properly. In time, the girl's love for her grandfather gives Grange Copeland his "third life." Whereas the first half of the book demonstrates how love can turn to murderous hatred, the second half shows how hatred can give way to selfless love.

For some critics, the second half fell flat, mostly in comparison to the harrowing tailspin that preceded it. A number of black readers had another complaint: They were disturbed by Walker's daring effort to explore the violence that sometimes occurs in a black family. White racist society is our real enemy, they scolded. Black writers must not portray their own people in an unfavorable light.

Walker would not stand for such criticism. Her own grandmother had been murdered by a man who claimed to love her, and wherever Walker looked she saw women taking abuse from men. Women make up half the world's population, she argued, just as people of color do, so "how can a family, a community, a race, a nation, a world, be healthy and strong if one half dominates the other half through threats, intimidation and actual acts of violence?" To put an end to the debate, she directed readers to the second half of her book, which shows how one man overcomes his worst impulses and grows to be a nurturing, loving individual.

Walker took solace amid this controversy in the many positive reviews she received. One that especially touched her came from the respected author Tillie Olsen, a long-time champion of women's rights. "Alice Walker," Olsen wrote, "is a major American writer, a cause for gratitude, delight and celebration." There had already been a major cause for celebration in Walker's home. Three days after she finished writing *The Third Life of Grange Copeland*, she gave birth to a daughter, Rebecca Grant.

Even as Walker nursed and diapered the baby, she somehow found time to serve as a writer-in-residence at Tougaloo College, where she taught from 1970 to 1971. As a teacher at Jackson State University, she had found it difficult to find interesting reading

Walker and her husband, Mel Leventhal, fuss over their daughter, Rebecca, in the summer of 1970. "There we were, working in Mississippi," Walker recalled. "I had a baby in one hand and my novel in the other."

material for her college students. The same problem confronted her at Tougaloo College. She wanted to use the works of black writers but lamented the fact that so many of their books were out of print.

While searching for reading materials that would interest her college students, Walker came across novels by Zora Neale Hurston and Nella Larsen that had long been out of print. The discovery caused her to face the limitations of her own education. Why hadn't her college teachers introduced her to these important writers? And why had their books been allowed to sink into obscurity? As she pondered these questions more and more, she felt a duty to reclaim their books, setting out on a determined crusade to uncover neglected black writers and woman writers who might speak to the hearts of her students.

Around this time, Walker began work on a new novel about the early days of the civil rights movement. To create a solid block of time during which to write, she made the difficult decision to place her one-year-old daughter in child care. Mrs. Cornelius, a neighbor who ran a nearby nursery school, agreed to take care of the toddler during the day, freeing Walker for a few hours of typing. But the novel came slowly, and she stayed depressed.

Receiving a fellowship from the Radcliffe Institute from 1971 to 1973 eased Walker's financial situation somewhat. Still, the pressure of her work, her baby, the novel, and the constant threat of violence combined to frustrate and exhaust her. Anyone could see that she needed some sort of break.

In 1972, Walker was offered a teaching position at Wellesley College, located on the outskirts of Boston, near her brothers. After talking it over with her husband, she decided to accept the post and take Rebecca north for a few months. Here was a chance, Walker thought, to build a course around neglected writers, to see some of her family members, and to be close enough to New York that she could visit old friends.

It was just a temporary job, a working vacation. She planned to return in the summer. But as her plane rose from the airport and turned above the oxbows and lazy curves of the slow delta rivers, Alice Walker was—except for a few brief visits—leaving Mississippi for good.

5

LIVING BY
THE WORD

❧

This portrait of Walker was taken in 1972, shortly after she left Mississippi to teach at Wellesley College. "If I had not gone and lived in Mississippi," she said later, "and had instead gone to live somewhere else where I could be free, I would never have been free."

WELLESLEY COLLEGE REMINDED Alice Walker of Sarah Lawrence College. Both were four-year liberal arts colleges for women, were set amid spreading trees and lovely courtyards, boasted a very selective admissions policy, and maintained such high academic standards that the students at each school considered themselves among the nation's elite.

The 28-year-old Walker arrived at Wellesley planning to introduce a course in women's studies that concentrated on the literature of female writers whose works had become neglected. Today, most colleges offer similar types of programs, but in 1972 the idea seemed quite radical. Only a progressive institution such as Wellesley would have given her permission to teach such a course.

She and her daughter, Rebecca, settled into a comfortable apartment near the Wellesley campus, and Walker began to make out a course list like none that the other professors had ever seen. Long-forgotten works such as Frances Watkins Harper's *Poems on Miscellaneous Subjects, Sketches of Southern Life,* and *Moses: A Story of the Nile*; Nella Larsen's *Quicksand* and *Passing*; and Ann Petry's *The Street* filled the page. Usually, Walker could not find enough of these out-of-print books for her students, so she resorted to making copies, which she stapled together and distributed to the class.

At first, her students did not know what to make of their novelist-teacher's ideas, but very soon they fell in love with the authors Walker taught. The English modernist Virginia Woolf and the New Orleanian Kate Chopin wrote movingly about the way social rules and obligations can tie a woman's hands. The poet Gwendolyn Brooks, the first black to be awarded a Pulitzer Prize, eyed the world with lyrical humor. And, Walker recalled, the way "the deep-throated voice of [antislavery activist] Sojourner Truth tends to drift across the room while you're reading" caused the students to marvel.

The woman writers Walker had chosen touched her students more than the male authors they read in their other classes. Never had they heard the viewpoints of women delivered with such grace and insistence. Gradually, Walker's students learned something they had never been taught before: The opinions and artistic expressions of women are as significant as those of men, and great black artists, like great white artists, speak movingly to all people. Judge for yourselves, Walker told them. Seek out the neglected works that speak deeply to you. Do not accept the biases that have filled bookshelves with the words of white men.

Among all these writers, Walker found a heroine, too. The novels of the Harlem Rennaissance author Zora Neale Hurston, which Walker had first encountered three years earlier, were so funny, poignant, tragic, and full of life that she wished she had written them all. Her favorites were the auto-biographical *Their Eyes Were Watching God* and *Mules and Men*, a novel that included many of the same folktales Walker had heard from her parents as a child.

In 1972, Walker was invited to lecture at the University of Massachusetts in Boston. Hurston's books excited Walker so much that she brought them to her brother Bill's house in nearby Dorchester, and they laughed and cried as they read them aloud after dinner. In the classroom, Walker said later, she "worried that Zora's use of black English of the twenties would throw some of the students off. It didn't. They loved it."

Hurston was a writer who could interest white teenagers and black workingmen alike, for she wrote about field hands, conjure women, preachers, and thieves in a way that made their stories seem vitally important. And she wrote in the dialect of the black southerners upon whom the characters were based. Walker loved the way Hurston "took the trouble to capture the beauty of rural black expression. She saw poetry where other writers merely saw failure to cope with English."

At last, Walker had found a mentor who wrote as she herself did. More than ever, she was deter-mined to bring Hurston's work—and that of other neglected woman writers—into the public eye. But first, she had to contend with her own writing—and the harsh northern winter. She worked on her novel during spare moments, trying to tie together the lives of several characters who come of age during the civil rights movement in the 1960s. But she seemed to spend most of her free time in bed, sick with the flu, as did Rebecca. It was a difficult winter.

Gradually, however, the dark mood that had burdened Walker since the death of Martin Luther

King, Jr., began to lift. Some of the short stories she had written in Mississippi were finding their way into magazines. Meanwhile, her publisher had agreed to bring out a second volume of poems. Walker missed her husband, but it was good to reap some of the rewards of her hard work in the South.

The real harvest came in 1973. In that year, Walker burst on the literary world with the publication of two books. The first was *In Love & Trouble: Stories of Black Women.* A collection of 13 short stories, several of which had been previously published in literary journals, it featured the tale she had written in college, "To Hell with Dying," as the final story.

In Love & Trouble, Walker said, was about "13 women—mad, raging, loving, resentful, hateful, strong, ugly, weak, pitiful and magnificent—[who] try to live with the loyalty to black men that characterizes all of their lives. For me, black women are the most fascinating creations in the world." Apparently, a number of literary critics thought so, too. The book proved to be an immediate success and went on to win the 1974 Richard and Hinda Rosenthal Foundation Award from the American Academy and Institute of Arts and Letters. Two stories—"Everyday Use," about the spiritual gap between country people and their children who run away to the city, and "The Revenge of Hannah Kemhuff," which owed a debt to Hurston's *Mules and Men* for its exploration of an old conjure woman's black magic—were chosen to appear in the *Best American Short Stories of 1973.*

Revolutionary Petunias & Other Poems, the second of Walker's two books to be published in 1973, contained many of the poems she had written during her years in Mississippi. She gave the book its unusual title after recalling that her mother, having taught her about the restorative power of flowers, always planted a profusely blooming petunia bush wherever they lived; her mother had also sent her a lavender petunia when Rebecca was born. "These poems," Walker noted at the start of the collection, "reflect . . . my growing realization that the sincerest struggle to change the world must start within. I was saved from despair countless times by the flowers and the trees I planted."

For Walker, flowers symbolize hope and determination in the face of hardship, and some of the best poems in *Revolutionary Petunias & Other Poems* read like instructions for living in difficult times. Other poems in the collection extend Walker's constant exploration of the poignant, hurtful, and moving moments of her life. Together they offer an impressionistic but highly personal history of her development. *Revolutionary Petunias & Other Poems*, which won the Southern Regional Council's Lillian Smith Award for poetry and garnered a nomination for the National Book Award, proved to be Walker's most critically successful book yet.

These two works were followed the next year by a book that was aimed at an entirely different readership. Eager to repay an old debt, Walker wrote a children's biography about her mentor Langston Hughes, who had died in 1967. She hoped that *Langston Hughes: American Poet* would introduce the poet's verse to a generation of readers who might otherwise never hear of him.

Walker took a break from her busy writing schedule when the school year ended in 1973, returning home to Mississippi that summer. There, she discovered that it was no longer necessary to fear for her family's safety. Her neighbors now considered Walker and her husband "outside agitators" rather than dangerous members of the community.

Her husband was the main reason why they had become accepted in Jackson. Mel Leventhal was currently handling the biggest lawsuit of his life, suing the city's school system in an attempt to force desegregation, and he had become a local celebrity because he appeared regularly on television news shows to discuss the progress of the case. With a confident grin, he told his wife that he wanted to give their daughter "a completely safe (racially) Mississippi for her sixth birthday."

Walker could hardly believe her eyes, but her husband's boast almost seemed to be coming true. Wherever she looked, she saw the results of the sacrifices made by civil rights workers. The Colored Only signs on public restrooms had been torn down; blacks and whites swam together at the beautiful Ross Barnett Reservoir; and most gratifying of all, blacks were running for public office and winning.

Satisfied that her family was safe at home, Walker undertook a pilgrimage in August that she had been considering for some time. She wanted to find the grave of Zora Neale Hurston. It bothered Walker that the residences of William Faulkner, Flannery O'Connor, and the South's other great white writers had been made into shrines, whereas a black writer she revered above all others was buried in an unmarked grave.

On one of the hottest days of the summer, Walker flew to Fort Pierce, Florida, and began to interview anyone there who might remember Hurston, who had moved to the town in February 1958, two years before her death. Some of the older folks remembered the Harlem Renaissance author; Hurston had spent her later years working in the area as a maid, schoolteacher, and librarian. They said Hurston had never made a fuss about having once been a celebrated writer, even though she was living in near-poverty when they befriended her.

Apparently, Hurston had made a number of good friends in the area. When she died of a heart attack

"When I found Zora Neale Hurston," Walker said of the gifted novelist and folklorist, "it was like seeing that we've always been on the frontier, and that we're really at home there." Walker subsequently devoted a great deal of her time to bringing Hurston's works to the attention of a new generation of readers.

on January 28, 1960, shortly after her 69th birthday, they had paid for a nice funeral. A tombstone had not been in their budget, however, and she was buried in an unmarked grave in a racially segregated cemetery, the Garden of the Heavenly Rest.

Guided by the directions of the people she had questioned, Walker tramped through the tall weeds of the overgrown cemetery in search of the most likely spot where Hurston might be buried. Before long, Walker's legs were scratched and swollen with insect bites, but she carried on until she found her heroine's gravesite. There she had a tombstone placed that reads:

Zora Neale Hurston
"A Genius of the South"
Novelist Folklorist
Anthropologist
1901 1960

With the tombstone taken care of, Walker flew home again, proud to have done the right thing for a writer she regarded as her literary ancestor. In fact, she accomplished more than that. She also wrote an essay about her trip, "Looking for Zora," and when it was published nationally in *Ms.* magazine in 1975, the article sparked renewed interest in Hurston's work.

Not content to let the matter rest, Walker began compiling an anthology of Hurston's best writings. The result of Walker's labors, *I Love Myself When I Am Laughing . . . & Then Again When I Am Looking Mean & Impressive: A Zora Neale Hurston Reader*, was published in 1979. This volume also spurred interest in Hurston's work, and all of her major novels have since been reissued in paperback. Her fiction is studied in literature courses all over the world, and thanks to the publication of Walker's essay and anthology, Hurston's literary reputation now seems assured.

Walker returned to Jackson feeling somehow that her work in the South was over. Her husband agreed that the major civil rights battles had been won. They had come to Mississippi determined not to leave until they felt safe. Strolling down the street, helping their daughter lick an ice cream cone, they laughed with the realization that they could finally go where they wished.

Walker's husband talked wistfully of returning to his boyhood neighborhood in Brooklyn, where the battle for civil rights was just beginning to heat up. Walker thought she might be able to get a job as an editor at Ms., which was based in New York City. It would be wonderful, they agreed, to return to the scenes of their youthful courtship. With that, they packed up their belongings and headed north, free at last. ❧

6

MERIDIAN

❧

WHEN ALICE WALKER arrived with her husband and daughter in New York in 1974, she discovered that St. Marks Place, where she had lived after college, had changed quite a bit. No longer a dingy street paced by aging immigrants and folk guitarists, it had become the eastern center of hippie culture over the past eight years. Rock music blared from every colorfully painted window, girls in bell-bottom jeans and with flower-painted faces strolled with dreamy-eyed, bare-chested boys. Civil rights protests had given way to marches against the Vietnam War, and often those marches turned into dizzying concerts in Washington Square Park.

Walker and her husband, both of them just turning 30, felt out of touch with the psychedelic era. They bought a brownstone house in the Park Slope section of Brooklyn that sat among a row of similarly stately homes on a broad, tree-lined street. Walker loved the brownstone because it had a backyard where she could grow flowers. She got along well with her neighbors because they too enjoyed their rose gardens and tidy plots of tomatoes.

After making his living in Mississippi by suing racist businessmen, Mel Leventhal was surprised to find more cases of racial discrimination in Brooklyn than he could handle. Walker landed a job at Ms., working as an editor. Three days a week, she caught the subway into Manhattan and went to her office, thumbing through manuscripts of fiction and poetry and deciding which ones to include in the next issue.

A photograph of Walker taken around the time she wrote Meridian, *her second novel. To write the book, she drew from her experiences in the South; there, she said, she "had to face up to the system that had almost done me in and had done in my father and so many of my people."*

Despite the tiring pressures of furnishing a new home, finding a school for Rebecca, and working as an editor, Walker devoted herself more than ever to writing. Stories that had come to her in Mississippi still filled her head. The enduring smile of a friend, the ribald laugh of a retired roadhouse singer, the languid gaze of an old flame sparked ideas that quickly found their way onto paper. She also wrote essays for *Ms.* about the neglected woman writers she loved. And every day she labored over her latest novel.

All went well for a year—or seemed to, on the surface. And then her marriage, which had survived so much fear and tension, fell apart. Walker has written movingly about some of the most harrowing, private moments of her life, but she has so far refused to discuss the breakup in print. She prefers to say simply that she and her husband, after eight years of marriage, decided to separate.

Many of the poems written during that time, however, shed some light on the pain of divorce. One of the poems is entitled "Never Offer Your Heart to Someone Who Eats Hearts," and another, "He Said:," is filled with resignation:

> He said: I want you to be happy.
> He said: I love you so.
> Then he was gone.
> For two days I was happy.
> For two days, he loved me so.
> After that, I was on my own.

Most of these poems ended up in Walker's third volume of poetry, *Good Night, Willie Lee, I'll See You in the Morning*, which was published in 1979. Each poem in the collection speaks of an effort to accommodate not just the pain of divorce but all that Walker had been through since her college years. "It was a time of barely holding on," she said later, "as I felt myself changing, and not always knowing how or why. These are the poems of breakdown and spiritual disarray that led me eventually into a larger under-standing of the psyche, and of the world."

Walker chose as the centerpiece for the book the death of her father, who had succumbed to his many "poor man's illnesses" in the winter of 1973. Walker had traveled home to Eatonton for his funeral, and during the services it had been hard for her to think of her father with good feelings. She remembered him as being so distant, so tired, so impatient. Then she watched her mother go to the coffin to touch Willie Lee Walker's hand for the last time. He and his wife had suffered together through the ugly poverty of sharecropping, had raised eight children, and had lived side by side through good and bad times.

Walker thought her mother might feel bitter about how hard her life had been, so she was stunned to overhear the old woman whisper words of love and forgiveness into the dead man's ear. "Good night, Willie Lee," Minnie Walker said, "I'll see you in the morning." Alice did not understand then what her mother meant; she was feeling her own pain too deeply. It was not until she collected the poems for the book that the healing power of forgiveness struck home, and she decided to turn the last words of one parent to another into the title.

Despite Walker's spirit of forgiveness, all was misery. She and her husband agreed to take turns raising their daughter; each would keep Rebecca for a year. With that, Walker said good-bye to her small family, to the home she had so recently furnished, and to her beloved garden. She moved into a similar brownstone not far away, where she could nurse her wounds in peace.

Depressed and in "spiritual disarray," Walker set out that winter on a journey through her past. Invited home to attend the March for Jobs in Atlanta on January 15, 1976, she decided to take the opportunity to visit hometown friends, then continue on to

Jackson, and even retrace her steps to Boston. Visiting schoolgirl haunts in Eatonton, Walker stopped to see her high school sweetheart, Taylor Reese, now married with children and a successful real-estate business. The two old friends shared an hour of reverie, while Reese's son played at their feet. Walker admitted that she still dreamed about Reese, and he chuckled warmly. "I haven't changed," he sighed.

In Jackson, Walker visited her former neighbor Mrs. Cornelius. News of Walker's divorce did not phase Rebecca's nursery school teacher. She reassured the anxious mother that, in spite of the breaking up of the family, Rebecca would turn out just fine.

In Boston, Walker stayed with her brother Bill, who was making plans to move back to Eatonton. His news came as a shock, but Bill simply waved his hand when his youngest sister asked him why. Beautiful Blue Hill Avenue, the street on which he lived in Dorchester, had become a slum, and racial tensions had reached the breaking point. Whereas people in the South had learned to live together, people in the North seemed to be growing apart. Bill had moved to Boston 20 years earlier to escape racial prejudice, and he was going back home for the same reason.

Returning to her lonely Brooklyn apartment, Walker must have felt as if she had lost all of her homes. The process of writing, she had learned, could save her from despair; her friends were kind; and her new flower garden promised hope. But none of them could make her happy. When she finally finished the novel she had been working on for five difficult years, dull relief was all she could register. She wrote:

> Now that the book is finished,
> now that I know my characters
> will live,
> I can love my child again.
> She need sit no longer
> at the back of my mind

the lonely sucking of her thumb
a giant stopper in my throat.

Meridian, Walker's second novel, was published
in 1976. The heroine of the book is Meridian Hill,
a young woman whose experiences echo those of
Walker's during the heyday of the civil rights movement. A poor farmer's daughter, Meridian has a baby
while still a teenager, wins a scholarship to Saxon
College (a thinly disguised version of Spelman College), and inexorably finds herself drawn into the
struggle for racial equality in the South.

Walker has written extensively about the civil
rights movement, both in poetry and prose; but
Meridian is probably her most considered account of
the day-to-day struggle. The book, she said in *In
Search of Our Mother's Gardens*, is about "the Civil
Rights movement, feminism, socialism, the shakiness
of revolutionaries, and the radicalization of saints."
Yet by carefully evoking the smell of dusty roads, the
sweet tastes of lazy picnics, and the raucous noise of
jail cells, she connects the reader to the hard work
that makes those high-flown ideas real. Meridian falls
in love with a fellow activist named Truman Held,
and Walker lavishes attention on their tumultuous
romance.

It is a bittersweet novel, in that Walker under-
stands how much the civil rights movement took out
of its participants. By the end of the book, Meridian
is still brave and committed to her ideals, but she is
so thin and sickly that she sometimes collapses,
temporarily paralyzed, on the street. Many of her
friends have died or are in jail; others are bitter,
unable to find a new cause to believe in.

As such, Walker's second novel showed her exploring new territory. In *The Third Life of Grange
Copeland*, she had bravely opened the doors of a
sharecropper's cabin, shining a spotlight on the vio-

lence that poverty can ignite. In *Meridian*, she had peeled back the heroic veneer of the civil rights movement, pointing out the scars its heroes suffered.

Among the best novels to emerge from the civil rights movement, *Meridian* was praised by most critics, who were quick to group Walker with Ernest J. Gaines, Toni Morrison, Ishmael Reed, and the other young black writers who had emerged from the civil rights era with a new and encompassing perspective on the black experience. The reaction of a reviewer in *Black Scholar* was typical, calling Walker's book "an extraordinarily fine novel . . . written in a clear, almost incandescent prose that sings and sears." That same journal later named *Meridian* one of the 10 best novels written in the 1970s.

In 1977, largely because of *Meridian's* success, Walker won a prestigious Guggenheim Fellowship, which allowed her to quit her job at *Ms*. For much of the year, she tried to get started on a historical novel but could not seem to make it work. Realizing that a change of scenery might help, the 34-year-old writer pulled up her roots in 1978 and moved to the West Coast. "I disposed of the house," she remembered, "stored my furniture, packed my suitcases, and flew alone to San Francisco (it was my daughter's year to be with her father), where all the people in the novel promptly fell silent—I think, in awe. Not merely of the city's beauty, but of what they picked up about earth-quakes." Walker remained in San Francisco just long enough to grow comfortable with its sophisticated but easygoing way of life. She loved the way people of all races and persuasions treated each other with bemused tolerance, learning from each other, caring for the city, living more freely than any community she had ever seen. Walker admired the precipitous hills, the mysterious fogs, the gardens that studded winding pathways. These are some of the reasons why, to this day, she keeps an address in San

Establishing herself on the literary scene at around the same time Walker did, author and editor Toni Morrison took a similar approach to the writer's craft: "My job is not to become anybody's creature, not the publisher's, not the critical establishment's, not the media's, not anybody's. I'm not doing anyone justice, not the women's movement, not the black movement, not novels, not anyone, if I toe the line."

Francisco. Moving there, Walker wrote, "was one of the best decisions I ever made. My spirit, which had felt so cramped on the East Coast, expanded fully."

There was, in fact, so much to see and do in the Bay Area that Walker could not concentrate on her new novel. She had recently made the acquaintance of a "writer and sometime political activist," Robert Allen, editor of *Black Scholar*. Together they began to look for a cabin in the rural hills of Mendocino County north of the city.

Eventually, they found a poet's paradise, which Walker described in *Living by the Word* as "a small house in the country that stood at the edge of a large meadow that appeared to run from the end of our deck straight into the mountains. The mountains, however, were quite far away, and between us and them there was, in fact, a town. It was one of the many pleasant aspects of the house that you never really were aware of this." The house was low and wide, with windows that stretched from floor to ceiling, overlooking an apple orchard and a meadow where horses grazed.

How did Walker intend to pay for her rural Eden? The funds from the Guggenheim Fellowship would

Walker tends her garden in Mendocino County, California. She moved to the West Coast in 1978 after residing for the previous four years in Brooklyn, New York.

stretch only so far, and the royalties from her books were not very large. She realized that she would have to travel and give lectures. But first she intended to do nothing except relax and enjoy her new home and her new romance.

"There were days and even months when nothing happened," Walker recalled. "Nothing whatsoever. I worked on my quilt, took long walks with my lover, lay on an island we discovered in the middle of the river and dabbled my finger in the water. I swam, explored the redwood forests all around us, lay out in the meadow, picked apples, talked (yes, of course) to trees."

Walker found in her new companion some of the best qualities of Mel Leventhal. Allen proved to be warm, supportive, "openly and spontaneously affectionate." Unlike her always overworked former husband, however, Allen was eager to travel and explore. During their first year together, for instance, they flew to Cuba and met with Huey Newton, a cofounder of the militant black revolutionary movement known as the Black Panther party. Newton and his wife, Gwen, had fled the United States after he was convicted of voluntary manslaughter and his two retrials ended in hung juries.

Romance, rest, and travel were just what the doctor ordered. Returning to her country home, Walker decided not to leave again until she had finished her third novel. She canceled her lecture trips and swore to make her money stretch as far as it could until the book was finished. She thought it would take five years.

Just as Walker settled down to write again, her daughter arrived for a two-year stay. Nervous that Rebecca, who was not yet 10 years old, would not like the rugged rural life, Walker scrambled to fix up the guest room—and subsequently related her concern in the poem "My Daughter Is Coming!":

My daughter is coming!
I have bought her a bed
And a chair
a mirror, a lamp
and a desk.
Her room is all ready
except that the curtains
are torn.
Do I have time to buy shoji panels
for the window?
I do not.
First I must WRITE A SPEECH
see the doctor about my tonsils
which are dying ahead of schedule
see the barber and do a wash
cross the country
cross Brooklyn and Manhattan
MAKE A SPEECH
READ A POEM
liberate my daughter
from her father and Washington, D.C.
recross the country
and present her to her room.
My daughter is coming!
Will she like her bed,
her chair, her mirror
desk and lamp
Or will she see only
the torn curtains?

Walker need not have worried. Rebecca, like her mother, found northern California a paradise.

Strolling about her property, dreaming of the fruit trees she would plant if she had the money, Walker felt that for the first time as an adult she could breathe freely. In California, she had rebuilt her shattered life, finding a new home, a new lover, and new friends. With the arrival of her daughter, her family life was once again complete. Turning back to the modest house that sat nestled among recently planted flowers, Alice Walker knew it was time to get back to work.

7

THE PURPLE FLOOD

THE IDEA FOR Alice Walker's historical novel had first arrived during a walk with one of her sisters. "I was hiking through woods with my sister Ruth," the author recalled in *In Search of Our Mother's Gardens*, "talking about a lovers' triangle of which we both knew." The conversation wandered through "illnesses, divorce, several moves, travel abroad, all kinds of heartache and revelations," and by the time the hike was over, Walker had begun to believe that the events of the triangle would make a good story.

While Walker was going through a divorce in New York and savoring the glamour of San Francisco, she had not been able to make the pieces of the story fit together. It was only when she finally settled down in the hills of northern California that the tale began "almost to write itself." In the morning, she helped Rebecca get ready for school, sat down to write from 10:30 A.M. to 3:00 P.M., then stopped for the day when her daughter came home. They shared a pot of tea, Rebecca talked about her school day as they cooked dinner, and afterward they walked or sat on the deck watching evening fog rise in the hollow. Walker has written that these "days passed in a blaze of happiness."

Walker and her daughter, Rebecca, share a relaxed moment in the early 1980s.

77

In 1981, while Walker lived the artist's life in California, her second book of short stories was published in New York. *You Can't Keep a Good Woman Down* features a collection of 14 tales that were written primarily during her difficult years in New York. The anger and confusion of those times bristle on the page. Some of the stories read more like essays than fiction; one is a two-paragraph prose poem; others swat viciously at rapists, pornographers, bigots of every stripe, and those who talk a good game but never seem to actually do anything.

Reviewing the book in the *New York Times*, author David Bradley complained that it was "flawed by unassimilated rhetoric, simplistic politics, and a total lack of plot and characterization." But *You Can't Keep a Good Woman Down* was not intended to satisfy readers who seek a well-rounded tale with a punchy moral. In writing this book, Walker vented anger and frustration that had been building for years. It is perhaps her most personal volume—and because she let her guard down, writing in the heat of the moment, many readers find it her most appealing work. Perhaps anticipating such a reaction, Walker dedicated the book "to my contemparies" and to those who insist "on the value and beauty of the authentic."

Meanwhile, Walker's historical novel continued to blossom. Using a literary technique that dates back to the first novels ever written, she decided to tell the story entirely in the form of letters. The correspondents are two sisters born into the same sharecropper's world in rural Georgia that Walker had written about so effectively before.

One of the sisters, Nettie, becomes a missionary in Africa and sends home beautifully detailed descriptions of her life abroad. The other sister, Celie, remains in the South. Her letters, written in black folk English, tell a riveting tale, and they open the book, instantly plunging the reader into the nightmarish world of the 14-year-old Celie with the words: "He never had a kine word to say to me."

Celie reveals that she is repeatedly beaten and raped by her stepfather, Alphonso, who sends away the two children she bears him. Alphonso then forces her to marry Albert, a cruel widower who beats and berates Celie so horribly that she does not dare speak his name; instead, she fearfully refers to him as Mr. ———— in her letters. Alone and afraid, Celie can bring herself to write about her ordeal solely to God.

Life slowly improves for Celie when Shug Avery, a dazzling blues singer and Albert's former mistress, arrives in town and moves into their house. Much of the novel's power lies in the manner in which the two women go about restoring each other's life. Celie takes care of an ailing Shug, cooking for her, brushing her hair, and making sure she rests. Shug, in turn, protects Celie from being abused. Shug also introduces her to the simple pleasures in life, such as when they walk in a field of flowers and Shug tells Celie that it angers God "if you walk by the color purple in a field somewhere and don't notice it."

Walker chose the phrase "the color purple" for the title of the novel and slowly but surely wove the threads of her story into a tale of reunion and redemption. By the novel's end, Celie has found the courage to become independent; Albert has developed a grudging admiration for his wife; and Celie has been reunited with her children and with Nettie. "I liberated Celie from her own history," the author later confided to *Newsweek*. "I wanted her to be happy."

Walker had planned to spend five years writing *The Color Purple*, but the story would not wait. Devoting all her energy to it, she actually finished the book in one year. When her companion Robert Allen came home on the day Walker finished, she

A family snapshot of Walker taken in 1984, on the heels of her success with The Color Purple. *The best-selling book won both the Pulitzer Prize and the American Book Award and confirmed its author as one of the nation's top writers.*

Walker gives a public reading of excerpts from The Color Purple *at a New York City auditorium in October 1985.*

threw herself into his arms at the front door. She had grown to love Celie, Shug, Nettie, and even Albert during the past months. Finishing the book felt like losing her best friends. Exhausted, jubilant, and sad, Walker cried in Allen's arms.

After sending the manuscript to her editor at Harcourt Brace Jovanovich, Walker took the time to relax and enjoy her flowers. By now, there were azaleas, camellias, a flowering crab apple, and, of course, her mother's favorite lavender petunias growing in the yard. Perhaps she knew how good the novel was, because when asked about it, she replied calmly, "It's my happiest book. I had to do all the other writing to get to this point."

Published in June 1982, *The Color Purple* caused an immediate sensation. *Newsweek* called the book "an American novel of permanent importance." *Essence* said it was "one of the great books of our time." And the *San Francisco Chronicle* claimed that the novel would "stand beside literature of any time and

place." Readers admired the unflinching eye Walker
had turned on the abuse Celie suffers at Albert's
hands, and they marveled at the way the author
gradually pulled her characters out of despair. What
is *The Color Purple*'s theme, one reviewer asked?
"Love redeems; meanness kills."

Immediately following the book's publication,
Walker was bombarded with requests for interviews
and speaking engagements. She did her best to com-
ply, appearing on television talk shows and university campuses and at literary luncheons across the
country. The pace of her travels only grew more
hectic when *The Color Purple* won the American
Book Award and then garnered the most prestigious
honor awarded to American writers, a Pulitzer Prize.

Walker's publishers rushed out a paperback edi-
tion, which like the original hardcover version became a runaway bestseller. Within two years, the
book had gone through 26 printings, and there were
nearly 2 million copies in circulation. No longer
would Walker have to struggle to make ends meet.
Like Celie and Shug in her novel, she had survived
the lean times to make of herself an American success
story.

It was then that the backlash began. Taking a
second look at *The Color Purple*, some critics flinched
at Walker's portrayal of men as brutal, lazy, and
selfish. "*The Color Purple* can make you see red,"
wrote columnist Earl Caldwell of the *New York Daily
News*. "That's especially true if you are a man and
happen to be black." Another reviewer said in *Newsweek* that Walker's men "are predatory at worst, idle
at best."

Walker had heard these claims before. Even her
first novel had sparked controversy over its rendering
of black men. In response, she explained, "I was
writing a woman's story. I have written novels in

which men were dominant, and I don't try to balance it one way. I try to tell about one or two characters so you know them."

But the assaults continued, until Walker had to admit she was stunned by the way some of the black male critics were behaving. "I wouldn't have expected such a pettiness," she said later. "You know, they have no identification with the struggle of women! That's shocking in a people who, I had always assumed, identified with every struggle for human rights in the world."

In June 1983, exactly a year after the publication of her novel, Walker traveled to China with a group of woman writers. The past year of skyrocketing fame had worn her out, and she was happy to get away from all the controversy for a while. On the opposite side of the world, far away from all the microphones and flashbulbs, she relaxed, strolling through the strangely uniform streets of Beijing, admiring the open smiles of people in the street, and meeting the legendary Chinese woman author Ding Ling. But even in China, Walker discovered, *The Color Purple* had caused a sensation. The novel had just been published there to great acclaim. When she wondered what the story of black sharecroppers in Georgia could mean to Chinese readers, an editor politely explained, "But Alice, it is a very *Chinese* story." After all, Walker realized, oppression and hope are at war all over the world.

When Walker finally returned to her rural home in California that summer, she spent part of her royalties in planting a hundred fruit trees around the property. In a journal entry, she wrote: "Bought snapdragon yellow paint for the privy. The walls will be yellow, to capture the sun and cheerfulness, and the seat will be marine blue." She took time out to meditate, to swim, to nap, dreaming once of spending a romantic afternoon with her old mentor Langston

Hughes, restored in her dream to the dashing 30-year-old poet he had once been.

Every day more mail arrived, begging for interviews and speeches. Walker by now had become not just a noted author but a celebrity. People wanted to know everything about her. With that thought in mind, her editor suggested that Walker collect a number of her essays in a book. Arranged to cover the various aspects of her life, the volume might serve as an autobiography of sorts, as a journal about her thoughts and most significant moments. Maybe it would satisfy readers who hungered to know more about the author of their favorite novel.

So, in the winter of 1983, Walker published *In Search of Our Mother's Gardens*, subtitled *Womanist Prose*. The first page of the book explains what she meant by the subtitle:

> **Womanist** 1. From womanish. (Opp. of "girlish," i.e., frivolous, irresponsible, not serious) A black feminist or feminist of color. From the black folk expression of mothers to female children, "You acting womanish," i.e., like a woman. Usually referring to outrageous, audacious, courageous or willful behavior. Wanting to know more and in greater depth than is considered "good" for one. Interested in grown-up doings. Acting grown up. Being grown up. Interchangeable with another black folk expression: "You trying to be grown." Responsible. In charge. Serious.

Another definition in the book reads:

> Loves music. Loves dance. Loves the moon. Loves the Spirit. Loves love and food and roundness. Loves struggle. Loves the Folk. Loves herself. Regardless.

In Search of Our Mother's Gardens fleshes out Walker's manifesto of "womanism" with essays about her favorite neglected writers, about the civil rights movement, about her childhood, and about her struggle with hardship and depression throughout her life. Most of the essays had been published in magazines over the past 15 years; taken together, they succeed as an autobiography, just as Walker had hoped. This

Walker attends the movie premiere of The Color Purple *at Eatonton's Pex Theatre on January 18, 1986. Accompanying the author to the ceremonies were her companion, Robert Allen (right and opposite page), and her daughter, Rebecca.*

book, too, became a best-seller but also made its author more of a celebrity than she had already been.

Walker thought she would try to begin work on a new novel in 1984, but that was not to be. The hotshot Hollywood movie producers Jon Peters and Peter Guber offered to buy the rights to *The Color Purple.* They said it would make a terrific movie. Walker was not so sure. She had seen how other important books had been turned into mush on screen and was not interested in seeing her novel treated so casually.

To discuss the matter, Walker convened a meeting of five woman friends who batted the idea back and forth all afternoon. At last, they agreed that it was worth the gamble. After all, they said, how many movies do you see about black people anyway? Here was a chance to tell Celie and Shug's inspiring story to a huge audience that would never bother to read a novel.

Steven Spielberg, who had already directed such blockbuster hits as *Jaws* and *Raiders of the Lost Ark,* chose to make the movie. Known as a master of

suspense and adventure, he wanted to try his hand at something completely different, an intimate family drama. But because he was new to that sort of story, he asked for Walker's assistance every step of the way. She wrote a draft of the screenplay but admitted she had not done it very well and cheerfully passed that chore to Dutch writer Menno Meyjes.

When the time came to cast the roles, Walker selected the young comedienne Whoopi Goldberg to star as Celie. Spielberg picked well-known actress Margaret Avery to play Shug and hired Adolph Caesar and Danny Glover for the lead male roles. Talk show host Oprah Winfrey rounded out the main cast.

Filming of the movie would not start for another year, so Walker returned home to select her best poems from the past several years for inclusion in her third volume of poetry, *Horses Make a Landscape Look More Beautiful*. Published in 1984, the collection focuses on the ways a person develops an artistic sensibility as a means of making sense of the world. Since her dark days in college, poetry had always helped save Walker from despair, and *Horses Make a Landscape More Beautiful* can be read as a solemn thank you to the imaginative spirit that keeps the poet alive.

Still unable to get started on a new novel, Walker planted hollyhocks in her burgeoning garden, traveled to Jamaica to visit reggae singer Bob Marley's gravesite at the tiny village of Nine Miles, and found herself writing letters to God, as Celie had done in *The Color Purple*. But whereas Celie pleaded with God for help, Walker wrote in blissful thanks: "You continue to amaze me! Yesterday after Joan arrived I went up to the studio to get tomatoes for visiting friends—there are so many, you've really outdone yourself! There is no doubt in my mind that I am blessed."

Filming of *The Color Purple* began in the spring of 1985. Walker traveled to North Carolina that June and spent a week and a half on location. Director Spielberg asked her advice on hundreds of details, from the kinds of pews to be used in the church scenes to the type of fruit jars in Celie's kitchen. Watching Adolph Caesar and Danny Glover perform the roles of Alphonso and Albert, respectively, Walker admitted that she felt a new sympathy for the male characters she had created, "because when I see them it's so clear that they're so miserable. And I feel so sorry for a person who has constructed a life of misery without fully examining it to find out that it's so miserable."

The movie premiered in New York City that Christmas to a chorus of cheers. Walker strode arm in arm with her sister Ruth Walker Hood and companion Robert Allen through the klieg lights and applause that greeted her arrival. But it was not until a few weeks later, in January 1986, that the full effect of Walker's new celebrity came home to her. Ruth had gone home to Eatonton to organize a special movie premiere for her sister at the old Pex Theatre, where the whole Walker family had gathered during her youth to watch movies in the segregated balcony.

The entire town pitched in to help. Purple crepe paper draped store windows; a banner reading WELCOME HOME ALICE WALKER stretched across the main street; and searchlights arced through the nighttime sky as the Walker clan paraded down a red carpet into Eatonton's lone movie house. Inside, every niche was filled with purple flowers. Walker marveled at the way black and white patrons alike stood to applaud her work. Much had changed for her since those days when the ushers had shunted black moviegoers off to the balcony. Her brother James, stunned by all the attention accorded his famous sister, remarked, "I never thought I would see something like this—not in my lifetime."

Moviegoers worldwide reacted to *The Color Purple* with a similar sense of wonder. While some found Spielberg's version of the novel too pretty, others responded with tears to Whoopie Goldberg's moving portrayal of the long-suffering Celie. The film was nominated for 11 Academy Awards, and all the publicity propelled the novel back onto the bestseller list. *The Color Purple* by now had become a global literary and film phenomenon, one which forever altered Walker's position in the world. The 42-year-old author would never again be seen as just another noted writer. From now on, she would be an instantly recognized celebrity, with all the privileges and demands that come with that sort of acclaim. ❧

8

A MORE ENCOMPASSING EMBRACE

———— ❧ ————

Walker returns to her old stamping ground, Spelman College, in 1990 with her companion, Robert Allen, and her friend Jacqueline Royster.

ONE OF THE more pleasant aspects of Alice Walker's newly won celebrity was how it affected the lives of those around her. The success of the movie premiere of *The Color Purple* in Eatonton inspired Ruth Walker Hood to establish a nonprofit organization for charitable and educational purposes, The Color Purple Educational Fund Foundation, Inc., "as a living memorial to her sister." In April 1986, the Eatonton-based foundation launched The Color Purple Educational Fund Foundation Scholarship program for students needing financial assistance to further their academic careers.

Walker's interest and financial support has made her a generous contributor to both the foundation and the scholarship program. The author has even gone so far as to "adopt" three elementary school children in Eatonton. She has agreed to grant money annually to these youngsters for clothes, books, and other necessities, right through high school and college, as long as they maintain an A average in conduct and a B average in their classwork.

One of the more frustrating things that happens to an international celebrity is that reporters suddenly want to know one's opinion about any topic that happens to cross their minds. After decades of being treated with scorn in some quarters, wary respect or outright neglect in others, Walker found herself bombarded with questions regarding her position on every issue from abortion to nuclear disarmament. Rather than responding with flip answers, she set out to carefully examine her stance on each of these topics, and in doing so wrote essays that gradually expanded to cover a wide range of topical issues.

Walker's writings of this period promoted the rights of the elderly, homosexuals, Native Americans, and animals. Yet rather than drearily list grievances and complaints, she enlivened each piece with personal anecdotes. She made the reader understand how this compassionate writer had been touched by an old neighbor in a nursing home, a gay pride rally in San Francisco, the trial of Indian activist Dennis Banks, and the arguments of vegetarians.

Since completing *The Color Purple*, Walker had been trying to get started on another novel, but ideas would not come. Then, one day, while taking out the garbage, her mind flashed on an image of an old man in a nursing home talking to a younger one. That picture became the germ of a story that over the next several years would expand into her most ambitious novel yet. Walker set out to accomplish no less than rewrite the past 500,000 years of human history.

Attempting such a task required more courage than she had ever needed before. Walker prayed and meditated in a yurt (a circular domed tent) in her yard, took strength from dreams in which her ancestors appeared with encouraging words, and even repainted her house with bright pictures of clouds, the sun, a turquoise ocean, and birds and snakes, to allow creative spirits free reign. Some days the story came easily; other days made her cry.

It was during one of these bad spells in the winter of 1987 that Robert Allen celebrated Walker's 43rd birthday by inviting her on a journey across the Pacific Ocean to the island paradise of Bali. Buying a flower-print jumpsuit with the help of her daughter, resting beneath coconut palms while Allen and Rebecca attended a tribal fire dance, writing a poem about a chicken crossing a road, and then enjoying a spicy chicken satay dinner, Walker soaked in the beauty of the tropical island.

She also pondered the advice of an Indian woman guru, who had told Walker not to worry about being depressed or suffering writer's block. The guru had said that sad times are part of life as much as happy times are, and that both are good and holy. These were healing words to a woman who had experienced cycles of aching depression since her teenage years. Walker told herself, "Just be, Alice. Being is sufficient. Being is All. The cheerful, sunny self you are missing will return."

Back in California that spring, Walker and Allen joined a demonstration against nuclear weapons at Concord Naval Weapons Station. Like many of the other marchers, they were jailed briefly. When a reporter asked Walker why she continued to demonstrate after a lifetime of marching and speaking out against injustice, she replied: "There are things that you really owe, I feel. If I weren't politically active, I would feel as if I were sitting back eating at the banquet without washing the dishes or preparing the food. It wouldn't feel right to me."

The following week, on June 12, 1988, Walker finished compiling her second book of essays, *Living by the Word*. She included most of her recent articles concerning human rights, expanding her definition of the term to include all living things under the sun.

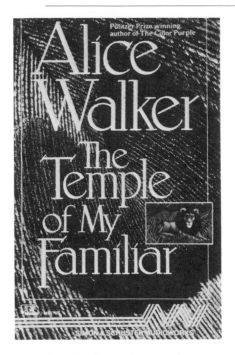

Poised in front of a microphone in a recording studio (opposite page), Walker makes her debut on audio cassette as she reads The Temple of My Familiar. *Published in 1989, Walker's fourth novel followed* The Color Purple *onto the best-seller list.*

In fact, one essay was entitled "Everything Is a Human Being."

Living by the Word also contained journal entries from Walker's years in northern California. These pieces show how her spirit had blossomed in the beautiful hills of Mendocino County. Responding to the book's generous tone, the *San Francisco Chronicle* praised her "willingness to share intimate details about her relationships with plants, animals, and intangible spirits."

At home, these same relationships came to play a large role in the writing of her fourth novel. Budding trees, neighborhood cats, and odd dreams found their way into a story that gradually expanded beyond 1,000 manuscript pages. As the novel took shape, Walker explained to an interviewer: "What I'm doing is literally trying to connect us to our ancestors. All of us. I'm really trying to do that because I see that ancient past as the future . . . If we can affirm it in the present, it will make a different future."

In a way, all of Walker's books attempt to connect old traditions to the present, to retell and correct stories that have become twisted over time. Each of her works might be read as an effort to incorporate the good and bad parts of American history into a tale that, rather than dividing people, leads them to understanding and compassion. But in her new novel, Walker dared to range across the whole of world history. That was one of the reasons why it took her six years to complete the manuscript, which was published in 1989 as *The Temple of My Familiar.*

Miss Lissie, the book's main character, is an enchanting, primal African goddess who, with the help of her friend Mr. Hal, recounts to Suwelo, a young college professor, various experiences from her hundreds of past lives. During these reminiscences, Miss Lissie refers to a pet that she owned, "a small,

incredibly beautiful creature that was part bird, for it was feathered, part fish, for it could swim and had a somewhat fish/bird shape, and part reptile." This fanciful animal, she explains, is a "beautiful little familiar, who was so cheerful and loyal to me, and whom I so thoughtlessly, out of pride and distraction, betrayed."

The "familiar" is just one of Walker's many unusual creations in this ambitious book, which reinvents human history as a sprawling drama that brings together cave men, rock stars, and even Celie and Shug Avery from *The Color Purple*. Relying on abrupt shifts between the past and the present to tell a story about personal relationships, Walker borrowed elements of Zora Neale Hurston's storytelling style, as well as those of Gabriel García Márquez and other South American "magical realists," in her effort to span countless centuries. The contemporary attitudes and strongly feminist political stance of the tale, however, are unmistakably her own.

Because *The Temple of My Familiar* was so unlike Walker's previous novels, it provoked a variety of responses. The *Los Angeles Times* called the book "a

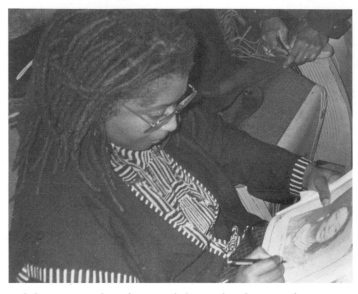

Walker signs her autograph for a fan. "It's so clear," she has pointed out, "that you have to cherish everyone . . . that every soul is to be cherished, that every flower is to bloom."

celebration of ordinary life and of everyday emotions," whereas South African novelist J. M. Coetzee said it "is a novel only in a loose sense. Rather, it is a mixture of mythic fantasy, revisionary history, exemplary biography and sermon." Author Isabel Allende saw in the book "the magic, the freedom, the beauty and the horror of dreams," while *USA Today*'s book critic was sure it would "by turns delight, shock, frustrate and inspire Walker's fans." Those fans turned out in droves for Walker's first novel since her blockbuster *The Color Purple*, and the new book became an instant bestseller.

For her next book, Walker collected all her poems in one volume. In a 1991 interview, she explained how strange it felt to piece the project together: "Compiling the collection was like going through a journal, yet poems feel different than journal entries. Examining the poems offered a chance to see whether I have been true to myself, and to see my life as almost that of an expatriate."

Walker entitled the collection *Her Blue Body Everything We Know: Earthling Poems 1965–1990 Complete*, with the words *blue body* referring to

Mother Earth. Harcourt Brace Jovanovich published the poems in 1991, the publishers going out of their way to produce a handsome volume that included a specially written introduction for each section by the author. The book also contains 16 new poems in addition to the poetry from her previous four volumes. Although Walker had learned a lot about writing since penning her first poems as a teenager, she decided not to rewrite any of her early verse for the collection, entrusting the reader to see the true heart beating behind her few awkward lines.

When a poet allows her work to be collected in a single volume, it is usually a sign that she wishes to reflect on what she has accomplished so far. Yet Walker had no intention of resting on her laurels. In 1991, her second children's book, *Finding the Green Stone*, was published. And in June 1992, just a year after the publication of *Her Blue Body Everything We Know*, her fifth novel, *Possessing the Secret of Joy*, was published.

Walker has also refused to rest on her other accomplishments, even though they are quite considerable. She has labored heroically in the civil rights movement, founded one of the first women's literature classes, launched a campaign to promote the work of neglected black and woman writers, and even become a publisher, of Wild Trees Press. Yet ever since she was told to move to the back of a bus while on her way to college, she has continued to speak out forcefully against injustice and cruelty wherever she sees it. She is now among the nation's leading literary speakers on the rights of the dispossessed.

The road from sharecropper's daughter to world-renowned author was by no means an easy one. But Walker prefers to look on the bright side of her experience. "In my development as a human being and as a writer," she explained in *In Search of Our Mother's Gardens*, "I have been, it seems

Walker and her daughter, Rebecca (far right), converse with a group of children at a reception for the Color Purple Educational Fund Foundation at Rock Eagle, Georgia. A nonprofit organization for charitable and educational purposes, the foundation was formed in 1986 by one of the author's sisters, Ruth Walker Hood, and features a program for students requiring financial assistance to further their academic careers.

to me, extremely blessed, even while complaining. Wherever I have knocked, a door has opened. Wherever I have wandered, a path has appeared. I have been helped, supported, encouraged, and nurtured by people of all races, creeds, colors, and dreams; and I have, to the best of my ability, returned help, support, encouragement, and nurture. This receiving, returning, or passing on has been one of the most amazing, joyous, and continuous experiences of my life."

Today, Walker's life continues to be "extremely blessed." She remains friends with her former husband, Mel Leventhal, who carries on his civil rights work in New York. She takes great pride in her daughter, Rebecca, who has been studying history at Yale. And she continues to live with her companion, Robert Allen, among the fruit trees and flowers in their northern California home.

Walker's collected poems conclude with an essay that has her sitting on her porch in Mendocino County, a continent away from her birthplace in Georgia. Morning fog rests like a lake in the valley; majestic hawks swoop and soar. She feels lucky to live in such beautiful surroundings but nostalgic for her childhood in Eatonton. Looking back at her life so far and imagining what is to come, Alice Walker reveals in "Once, Again," the book's last poem, the happiness and peace she has found after nearly five decades of hard traveling:

> Once again simple
> Once again childlike
> The poem opening out
> Into the grass. ❧

APPENDIX: BOOKS BY
ALICE WALKER

1968   *Once*

1970   *The Third Life of Grange Copeland*

1973   *In Love & Trouble: Stories of Black Women; Revolutionary Petunias & Other Poems*

1974   *Langston Hughes: American Poet*

1976   *Meridian*

1979   *Goodnight, Willie Lee, I'll See You in the Morning; I Love Myself When I Am Laughing . . . & Then Again When I Am Looking Mean & Impressive*

1981   *You Can't Keep a Good Woman Down*

1982   *The Color Purple*

1983   *In Search of Our Mother's Gardens: Womanist Prose*

1984   *Horses Make a Landscape Look More Beautiful*

1987   *To Hell with Dying*

1988   *Living by the Word*

1989   *The Temple of My Familiar*

1991   *Finding the Green Stone; Her Blue Body Everything We Know: Earthling Poems 1965–1990 Complete*

1992   *Possessing the Secret of Joy*

CHRONOLOGY

—————— ❧ ——————

1944   Born Alice Malsenior Walker on February 9 in Eatonton, Georgia

1952   Loses sight in right eye from a BB gun accident

1961   Elected prom queen and graduates from high school as valedictorian; enrolls at Spelman College on a scholarship

1962   Serves as a delegate to the World Youth Peace Festival in Helsinki, Finland

1963   Transfers to Sarah Lawrence College

1964   Travels through Africa and Europe; writes "To Hell with Dying"

1965   Graduates from Sarah Lawrence College; becomes a voter registration volunteer in Liberty County, Georgia; moves to New York City and becomes a staff worker for the city's Department of Welfare

1966   Awarded a fellowship from the Bread Loaf Writer's Conference

1967   Awarded a fellowship from the MacDowell Colony; marries Melvyn Rosenman Leventhal; wins first prize in the annual *American Scholar* essay contest for "The Civil Rights Movement: What Good Was It?"; first short story, "To Hell with Dying," is published; moves to Jackson, Mississippi; becomes a consultant on black history to the Friends of the Children of Mississippi

1968   Walker becomes a writer-in-residence at Jackson State College; first poetry collection, *Once*, is published

1969   Awarded a grant from the National Endowment for the Arts; daughter, Rebecca Grant, is born

1970   Becomes a writer-in-residence at Tougaloo College; first novel, *The Third Life of Grange Copeland*, is published

1971   Awarded a Radcliffe Institute fellowship

1972   Becomes a lecturer in literature at Wellesley College and the University of Massachusetts, Boston

1973   Places a tombstone at Zora Neale Hurston's gravesite; *Revolutionary Petunias & Other Poems* is published, wins the Southern Regional Council's Lillian Smith Award for poetry, and is nominated for the National Book Award; first short story collection, *In Love & Trouble*, is published

1974   Walker moves to New York City; becomes an editor at *Ms.* magazine; *In Love & Trouble* wins the Richard and Hinda Rosenthal Foundation Award from the American Academy and Institute of Arts and Letters; *Langston Hughes: American Poet* is published

1976   Walker divorces Melvyn Leventhal; *Meridian* is published

1977   Walker awarded both Guggenheim and MacDowell Colony fellowships

1978   Moves to San Francisco, then to Mendocino County in northern California

1979   *Goodnight, Willie Lee, I'll See You in the Morning* is published

1981   *You Can't Keep a Good Woman Down* is published

1982   Walker becomes a professor at both the University of California, Berkeley, and Brandeis University; *The Color Purple* is published

1983   *The Color Purple* is awarded the American Book Award and the Pulitzer Prize; Walker's first essay collection, *In Search of Our Mother's Gardens*, is published

1984   *Horses Make a Landscape Look More Beautiful* is published

1985   Walker advises Steven Spielberg in the filming of *The Color Purple*

1986   Attends Hollywood-style premiere of *The Color Purple* at Eatonton's Pex Theatre

1987   *To Hell with Dying* is published

1988   *Living by the Word* is published

1989   *The Temple of My Familiar* is published

1991   *Finding the Green Stone* and *Her Blue Body Everything We Know* are published

1992   *Possessing the Secret of Joy* is published

FURTHER READING

Baker, Houston A., Jr. *Black Literature in America*. New York: McGraw-Hill, 1971.

Banks, Erma Davis. *Alice Walker, an Annotated Bibliography 1968–1986*. New York: Garland, 1989.

Bloom, Harold, ed. *Alice Walker*. New York: Chelsea House, 1989.

Butler-Evans, Elliott. *Race, Gender, and Desire: Narrative Strategies in the Fiction of Toni Cade Bambara, Toni Morrison, and Alice Walker*. Philadelphia: Temple University Press, 1989.

Christian, Barbara. *Black Women Novelists*. Westport, CT: Greenwood, 1980.

Cooke, Michael G. *Afro-American Literature in the Twentieth Century*. New Haven: Yale University Press, 1984.

Evans, Mari, ed. *Black Women Writers*. Garden City, NY: Doubleday, 1984.

Geuder, Patricia A. *The Color Purple*. New York: Hearthstone, 1987.

Lanker, Brian. *I Dream a World: Portraits of Black Women Who Changed America*. New York: Stewart, Tabori & Chang, 1989.

Pratt, Louis H. *Alice Malsenior Walker*. Westport, CT: Meckler, 1988.

Rummel, Jack. *Langston Hughes*. New York: Chelsea House, 1988.

Walker, Alice, ed. *I Love Myself When I Am Laughing . . . & Then Again When I Am Looking Mean & Impressive: A Zora Neale Hurston Reader*. New York: Harcourt Brace Jovanovich, 1979.

Witcover, Paul. *Zora Neale Hurston*. New York: Chelsea House, 1991.

INDEX

PICTURE CREDITS

Robert Allen: p. 74; A/P Wide World Photos: pp. 3, 28, 34, 40, 84,
92–93; Black Archives, Florida A & M University: p. 64; Color Purple
Foundation: pp. 94, 96; Courtesy of Georgia Department of Archives
and History: pp. 20–21, 24; Bernice B. Perry, Photographer, from the
Collection of The MacDowell Colony: pp. 44, 47; Collection of the
Research Libraries of The New York Public Library: pp. 49, 50; Sarah
Lawrence College/Office of Publications: pp. 12, 16, 17; Schomburg
Center for Research in Black Culture, New York Public Library, Astor,
Lenox, and Tilden Foundations: pp. 18, 37, 49, 73; Spelman College
Archives: pp. 2–3, 30–31, 88; UPI/Bettmann: pp. 10, 54, 80; Courtesy
of Alice Walker: pp. 23, 26, 76, 79, 85; Wellesley College: 56, 67

TONY GENTRY, whose poetry and fiction have been widely published, is also the author of *Paul Laurence Dunbar*, *Dizzy Gillespie*, and *Jesse Owens* in Chelsea House's BLACK AMERICANS OF ACHIEVEMENT series. An honors graduate of Harvard College, he holds a degree in history and literature and is currently attending graduate school at New York University.

NATHAN IRVIN HUGGINS, one of America's leading scholars in the field of black studies, helped select the titles for the BLACK AMERICANS OF ACHIEVEMENT series, for which he also served as senior consulting editor. He was the W.E.B. Du Bois Professor of History and of Afro-American Studies at Harvard University and the director of the W.E.B. Du Bois Institute for Afro-American Research at Harvard. He received his doctorate from Harvard in 1962 and returned there as a professor in 1980 after teaching at Columbia University, the University of Massachusetts, Lake Forest College, and the California State University, Long Beach. He was the author of four books and dozens of articles, including *Black Odyssey: The Afro-American Ordeal in Slavery*, *The Harlem Renaissance*, and *Slave and Citizen: The Life of Frederick Douglass*, and was associated with the Children's Television Workshop, National Public Radio, the Boston Athenaeum, the Museum of Afro-American History, the Howard Thurman Educational Trust, and Upward Bound. Professor Huggins died in 1989, at the age of 62, in Cambridge, Massachusetts.